Careers in Gr   cations
A R

Sally An

GATFPress

Pittsburgh

Copyright 1998
Graphic Arts Technical Foundation
All Rights Reserved

Library of Congress Catalog Card Number: 97-74137
International Standard Book Number: 0-88362-209-2

Printed in the United States of America

GATF Catalog No. 1546

Reproduction in any means without specific permission is prohibited.

Product names are mentioned in this book as a matter of information only and do not imply
endorsement by the Graphic Arts Technical Foundation.

GATF*Press*
Graphic Arts Technical Foundation
200 Deer Run Road
Sewickley, PA 15143-2600
Phone: 412/741-6860
Fax: 412/741-2311
http://www.gatf.org

Orders to:
GATF Orders
P.O. Box 1020
Sewickley, PA 15143-1020
Phone (U.S. and Canada only): 800/662-3916
Phone (all other countries): 412/741-5733
Fax: 412/741-0609
Email: gatforders@abdintl.com

GATF*Press* books are available at quantity discounts for schools, corporations, and associations.
Contact Peter Oresick at 412/741-6860 for details.

Printed on 70-lb. Roosevelt Offset Enamel

Table of Contents

Publisher's Foreword

Welcome to the world of graphic communications—one of the largest industries in the United States today. The Graphic Arts Technical Foundation, as part of its mission to serve the field as a leading resource for technical information, is pleased to offer this book, designed to help a student make a career choice in an industry with almost endless career possibilities.

Graphic communications, or printing, is a growth industry that uses a variety of printing processes to manufacture a variety of products, from cereal boxes to books to T shirts. This book provides an overview of the different printing processes and the major printing markets. It then describes approximately 15 different occupations within graphic communications, giving the reader a flavor of the diversity of the industry. The book also lists numerous sources of assistance for the prospective new member of the field—schools offering degrees in graphic communications, industry associations, books and magazines on the subject, and home pages to visit for more information. Also included is an extensive glossary to help newcomers understand industry jargon.

After reading this book and speaking with people already working in the industry, we hope you will select one of the many occupations within graphic communications as your career path.

If that occupation requires a college education, consider contacting the National Scholarship Trust Fund (see p. 75). NSTF, housed at GATF, administers the largest scholarship program for the graphic communications industry. A scholarship from NSTF could help make your career in graphic communications a reality.

Please feel free to contact me (POresick@gatf.org) with comments and suggestions about this book. We will revise it every three years to keep it up-to-date. In the meantime, visit our website at www.gatf.org for the latest information about this dynamic industry.

Peter Oresick
Director, Technical Information and Education Programs
GATF

Acknowledgments

My thanks to Peter Oresick, director of technical information and education programs at GATF, for suggesting and guiding me through this project. It was a great opportunity to learn so much about the graphic communications industry and get an inside look at what still seems to me to be a magical process. Special thanks also to Pamela Groff at GATF, and to Laura Shefler, Robert Ham, and Mavis Milne for their encouragement and intelligent reading of the manuscript.

There were many men and women who took the time to explain the industry and talk to me about their work. Many thanks to Tom Daly, Josette Lankevich, and Tim Stratman at R.R. Donnelley & Sons; Glen Ketchian, Kay Mensing, Jim Fink, Tom Orr, Ron Solei, Jeff Chamberlin, and Lloyd LaMotte at Banta; Bill Schleier and Jerry Williamson at Williamson Printing Corporation; Jeff Waterhouse, Dave Mohr, Shane McPherson, and Brian Schlifke at American Color; Mike Kane of Benshoff Printing; Timothy Ludtke of Stevenson Photo Color Company; Chet Miller of Herlin Press; William Brennan of Presstar Printing Corporation; Stu Gallup of A. B. Dick Company; Kevin Canepa of Edwards Brothers; Michael Jorgensen and Jimmy Proulx of Impressions Incorporated; Eric Neumann of Rochester Institute of Technology; Tony Stanton, director, graphic communications management, Carnegie Mellon University; Dan Wilson, assistant professor of printing and publishing technology, Pennsylvania College of Technology; and the following GATF employees: George Ryan, president; John Sweeney, vice president; Hal Hinderliter, director of the Center for Imaging Excellence; and Frank Benevento, faculty emeritus, of GATF.

Finally, thanks to all those who reviewed this manuscript:

- Manfred Breede, professor of printing processes, Ryerson Polytechnical Institute
- Howie Fenton, senior technical consultant/digital technology, GATF
- Dee Gentile, information officer, GATF
- Len Mogel, founding publisher of *National Lampoon* and other magazines
- Vicki Stone, Green Printing Company
- Richard Warner, vice president and director of research, GATF
- Frances Wieloch, editor, *GATFWorld*
- James Workman, director, training programs, GATF

Sally Ann Flecker
Pittsburgh
April 1998

Chapter 1

Getting Acquainted

What Is Graphic Communications?

Take a good look around you.
Wherever you are as you read this—sitting on a hard chair at the library, browsing at the bookstore, bumping along on the bus, or lounging on your living room couch—you are surrounded by graphic communications. This book, for instance, is a product of one of the largest parts of the graphic communications industry—book printing.

But book printing is only one aspect of the graphic communications industry. Keep looking around you. Almost everywhere you set your eyes you see other examples of graphic communications. The poster on your wall. The liner notes from your latest CD. The morning newspaper. The empty potato chip bag. The birthday card that came in today's mail. (And those crisp green bills inside the card!) The phone book. A memo pad. Soda cans. A mac-and-cheese box. Your favorite magazines. The photocopied map with directions to Saturday night's party. Even the lottery ticket you bought on your way home.

We've got you surrounded.

Graphic communications is what is often referred to as the printing industry. But with more and more printers now offering electronic products and services as a complement to their more traditional lines, graphic communications better describes the work of today's industry.

If you were reading a textbook right now, it would tell you that graphic communications involves the production and dissemination of text and images by printed or electronic means. Still, that's a dry explanation for a pretty amazing process.

So imagine this: You have a painting of your favorite scene—the mountains in Colorado or the clearing along the river that no one but you seems to have discovered.

And you want to reproduce this painting so you can send copies of it to, say, 25,000 of your favorite friends.

The catch is that printing hasn't been invented yet. You could have the best paints, colored pencils, inks, brushes—and all the free time in the world. But you could never make 25,000 copies.

In fact, even one copy is probably out of the question. It might be nigh on impossible to reconstruct precisely the vividness of the painting—the subtle shadings in the blue sky, the 25 different greens on the hillside, the splash of red over in one corner.

Yet making exact, detailed reproductions of paintings, photographs, illustrations, and words is everyday business in the graphic communications industry. Printers, following a series of processes based on time-tested principles, can make such a precise copy that you'll be hard pressed to tell which is the original.

It's not magic. But it is remarkable. One of the riddles of life is that the things that are most remarkable are exactly those that someone has been able to make look natural and effortless. What is more simple and more marvelous, for instance, than Michael Jordan jumping to make a basket? So look around you again. Pick up any one of the printed products within arm's reach, take a good look at it, and begin to imagine the skilled and innovative work that went into making it look sharp and professional.

By the way, the lion's share of work in the graphic communications industry refers to printing words and images on paper. But printing can also happen on metal, glass, plastic, textiles, and other surfaces. And of course, the graphic communications industry is becoming equally at home working with new media products—CD-ROMS, interactive software, and Internet and Web sites.

So whether you're at your computer or out and about in the world, graphic communications products are all around you.

A Sure Choice

If you want to know why this is a good time to choose graphic communications as a career, try this little experiment, a sort of one-room scavenger hunt. Pick a room in your house at random. Find all the printed items in the room—the pizza box, the Publishers Clearinghouse announcement, your driver's license—and read them out loud. If it doesn't take you a good long time to cover everything, well, you must be living where your nearest neighbors are elks and caribou.

The point here is that the graphic communications industry is a huge one. For sheer numbers, the restaurant industry has the highest number of establishments in the United States. But printing and publishing companies combined are right behind. And just as most towns have at least one restaurant, printing companies—from the very small to the very large—can be found in cities and towns all across the country.

So there's plenty of work—in plenty of places—in the graphic communications industry. Whether you want to live on the East Coast or the West Coast, whether it suits you to work in a buzzing metropolis or out in the sticks next to a

cow pasture, you can find a printing facility or office that fits the way you want to live and the part of the country you want to settle in.

Another reason why this is a good time to choose graphic communications as a career is that the industry is a long-established one. Right now, it is experiencing moderate growth, and that is expected to continue.

A recent survey showed that three out of five printing firms were actively recruiting employees. The tremendous demand for new employees isn't a trend that is going to die down any time soon. By one estimate, as many as 35,000 to 50,000 jobs at all levels of the industry are available right now. Many printing companies are having a difficult time finding enough workers with the skills and knowledge necessary for a modern-day operation.

If you're looking for a steady career with plenty of opportunity, graphic communications is the one.

An Industry on the Electronic Frontier

Stability and opportunity. But you want even more out of your career. You want an interesting job, one that you can sink your teeth into. Well, plain and simple, graphic communications is an exciting place to be these days. For one thing, digital technology is transforming the way that work gets done in a printing operation. Craftsmanship is still important. But the tools of the craftsman have changed completely. The X-Acto knife is giving way to mouse and monitor. Printing plates can be bypassed completely with a new technology called direct-to-press. In fact, the latest generation of cameras is digital. Film doesn't even enter into the picture, so to speak.

As many as 35,000 to 50,000 jobs at all levels of the industry are available right now.

And there's a pioneering spirit these days in graphic communications as companies begin to explore interactive digital media—CD-ROMs, the Internet, and the World Wide Web. The graphic communications industry is uniquely poised to tap into these new mediums and reap their rewards. This means that there is a lot of spirited and innovative work being done. Printing houses are ripe with possibility and full of excitement and challenge.

Taking in the Sights

A good career book should be like a travel guide. It can give you a glimpse of a world you haven't been to yet, prepare you for your journey, show you the best ways to get there, and offer tips for the most satisfying experience.

In this book, we'll show you the "sights" of the graphic communications industry.

Background

Before you travel to a foreign country you want to know something about the place and the culture. How big is it? How many people live there? How technologically advanced is it? Chapters 2 and 4 will offer an overview of graphic communications. You'll learn about the range of products made by the industry and the processes involved as well as be introduced to some of the market segments that make up the industry.

Economic snapshot

Before you choose a career, you will want to know the industry outlook. What are its projections for growth? What's the prognosis for employment opportunities? We'll let you know what's hot and what's not in Chapters 3 and 6.

History

Graphic communications has roots that stretch back thousands of years. Chapter 5 offers a short history of the industry and lets you know about the ways that printing and graphic communications have shaped modern civilization.

Picture yourself here

Chapters 7, 8, 9, and 10 offer snapshots of some of the technical and professional roles that are possible in this field. Here's what you'll be looking for: What kind of work is involved? Who is this role especially suited for? What skills, abilities, and traits does this role require?

As various roles are explained, we'll describe the imaging, printing, and finishing processes that work hand in hand to create a graphic communications product—whether it is the printed piece that has been the industry's traditional territory or the Internet site that is rapidly becoming another facet of the business.

Graphic communications is, at heart, a creative undertaking that is part and parcel of a highly innovative and technical business. Many of the top graphic communicators—highly skilled press operators, electronic prepress experts, sales people, and educators—say that they were drawn to the industry because it gave them a way to use and develop their technical skills as well as their artistic sensibilities.

What's the next step? Is graphic communications sounding more and more like a good career choice for you? If so, be sure to check out Chapter 11. Here you can get a heads up on what employers are looking for. Find out what kinds of traits, skills, and knowledge will make you an attractive candidate for a job in the industry. In this final section of the book, we'll also provide lists of schools, associations, and other resources to help you learn more about the field of graphic communications.

What You Should Know About:
The Printing Process

Lay of the Land

Printing can take place on a variety of surfaces—everything from paper, cloth, and metal to glass, wood, and cardboard. You are used to seeing printing on flat surfaces like paper or fabric as well as on three-dimensional surfaces such as packages and bottles. But you may not have given much thought to the special processes that are involved. There are five different kinds of printing processes, each able to tackle a different kind of job. Each process requires the use of specialized equipment, inks, and finishing equipment. It also requires expertise on the part of its press operators, sales force, customer service representatives, prepress and bindery specialists. In this section we'll give you a quick rundown of each process and its particular uses.

Lithography

Water and oil don't mix

That's the basic principle behind the most commonly used printing process—lithography. Lithography is top dog in the graphic communications industry. About 60% of the work in the industry is lithographic. Print advertising, such as point-of-purchase displays and posters, as well as books, magazines, catalogs, directories, brochures, annual reports, even reproductions of paintings, are produced with the lithographic process.

Although it's based on a simple premise, lithography is a complicated process. Lithography requires a thin, flat printing plate that is usually made from metal. This plate is treated with photosensitive chemicals. The next step is a photographic process. The plate is covered with a film negative that has been made of a poster, perhaps, or pages for a magazine. It is then exposed to a special, intense light.

When that happens an image is left on the printing plate. If you're working with a negative, light has passed through the areas where the image is. When the light passes through the negative, it hardens the photosensitive material on the printing plate, creating the image you want to print.

The photosensitive substance that remains in the non-image areas of the plate—the places where you don't want any images or words—must be washed away. Now you're ready to print. And this is where the fact that water and oil don't mix becomes important.

The hardened part of the printing plate with the images is receptive to the inks, which are oily substances. The non-image areas are exactly opposite. They are receptive to water, and therefore repel the oily ink. The ink, then, is drawn to the image areas. And water (actually a more complex solution called dampening or fountain solution) keeps the nonimage areas free from the oily inks.

These days, most lithography is done using what is known as an offset method. In fact, lithography is so closely associated with this method of indirect printing that you will often hear lithography referred to simply as offset printing. The principle behind offset printing is simple: the inked image on a press plate is first transferred to another surface, most often a rubber blanket. The blanket, in turn, prints the inked impression onto a substrate, which could be paper, cardboard, or a variety of other surfaces.

Hudson-Sharp Model A-4 press; one of the first common impression cylinder presses (first was about 1935). Built in

Letterpress

Think Gutenberg

Letterpress, which dates back centuries, was the first printing process to be used commercially. Its use has declined over the last thirty years as lithography has become more cost-effective. Still letterpress continues to hold a small but significant place in the print industry. Letterpress accounts for about 5% of all printing done today.

Letterpress is a less complex process than lithography. It is often referred to as a relief process, which means that the image is printed using a raised surface. Here's how it works: the image, let's say a letter of the alphabet, is molded or carved onto one form. This creates an area that is raised above the non-image area. This image area is inked, then pressed against another form that holds the paper or other material where it leaves the printed impression.

Copperplate press in use in 1645.

Flexography

Darwin would have approved

One of the striking cases of evolution in the printing industry has been the development of a process called flexography. Flexo, as it is often shorthanded in the industry, is a cousin to the letterpress process of printing. Flexography works with a raised image to print in the same way that letterpress does.

There's a crucial difference between the two processes, though. That difference lies with their printing plates. In letterpress, the typeforms that carry the raised image areas are rigid. In flexography, as you might have already guessed, these typeforms are flexible—molded out of rubber or plastic. That flexibility makes this process a great choice for printing on surfaces as diverse as corrugated cardboard, folding cartons, plastic film, and wrapping paper.

Packaging (for instance, packing cartons as well as the stand-up pouches you find on grocery store shelves) and pressure-sensitive labels are two of the most prominent end uses of flexographically printed products. Flexographic presses are also becoming more widely used in newspaper publishing as many papers begin to use some color on formerly black-and-white pages.

Use of flexography is expanding, propelled by its improving quality, affordable cost, its ability to operate at high press speeds, and the relative simplicity of the process. A recent marketing trend places even more emphasis on packaging as a way to reach buyers, which bodes well for the flexographic process. Insiders expect the market to change rapidly and say that flexography is the technology to watch.

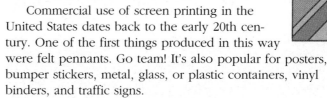

Gravure

The long run

Gravure is the printing process of choice when you need to print, say, a few million copies. This process, which prints images that have been engraved or etched into a surface,

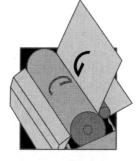

has been around for more than 200 years. The charms of gravure include the high quality of its images and its ability to maintain that quality and consistency over extremely long pressruns. It currently commands 16% of the work in the industry, and it is used in the printing of catalogs, commercial magazines, packaging, specialty work such as wallpaper and floor coverings, Sunday newspaper supplements, calendars, postage stamps, and fine art reproductions.

Although the quality of gravure has always been stunning—colors are vivid and dense—gravure has become more prominent over the last two decades as it has become faster and more cost-effective. A state-of-the-art gravure press can print up to 144 pages per revolution at speeds exceeding 50,000 revolutions per hour. Some of the largest presses in the world are gravure presses that can handle paper as wide as 125 inches. What made gravure a slow process before was the work that went into preparing the plates for press. Cylinder preparation was slow and expensive for this "below the surface" printing process. Originally, gravure cylinders had to be chemically etched or mechanically engraved to form the image. These days, a direct-digital engraving process, involving computers and lasers, can do the job much more quickly.

Screen Printing

Small but mighty

Screen printing, an ancient printing technique practiced in early China, Egypt, and Japan, accounts for 2% of the dollar volume in the graphic communications industry. But it's an important 2%. With screen printing, an image can be produced on just about every shape or surface—curved or vertical, hard or soft.

Commercial use of screen printing in the United States dates back to the early 20th century. One of the first things produced in this way were felt pennants. Go team! It's also popular for posters, bumper stickers, metal, glass, or plastic containers, vinyl binders, and traffic signs.

Here's how it works: Material (silk used to be the fabric of choice, hence you'll sometimes hear it called silk screening) is stretched across a frame, which can be huge or miniature. A stencil (these days a photostencil that is made of light-sensitive coatings that harden when exposed to ultraviolet light) is applied that protects the nonimage areas. Ink is then forced through the open, or image, areas of the stencil onto the surface of the paper, film, or other substrate. To force it through, a rubber blade called a squeegee is used. (If you've ever cleaned a windshield, you get the idea.) That's the basic process.

There are a few things that make screen printing an attractive printing process. It's an easy process, even more so now that it can be fully automated. The ink is strong and durable. Printers can get up to one hundred times the thickness of ink in screen printing than with other processes, if the design of the product calls for it. And the process is about as versatile as they come. No other process can handle unwieldy materials the way screen printing can.

With increasingly sophisticated devices and techniques, screen printing will continue to be an attractive alternative for certain commercial printing applications.

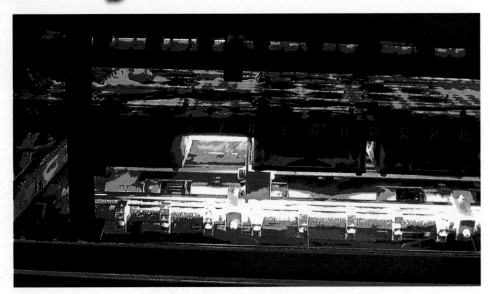

and then printed on the other side. In a perfecting press, both sides of a sheet are printed during the same run through the press. The chain grippers deliver the sheets to the stack where a jogging system gently aligns them as their journey comes to a close.

For some papers and inks, a powder is sprayed as each sheet is delivered. This very light dusting prevents ink from smearing or setting off on the back side as it comes into contact with the previous sheet.

Sheetfed presses accommodate paper as small as 10×15 inches and as large as 54×77 inches.

Sheetfed Printing Presses

The sheet goes on

You will hear two types of printing systems mentioned in the industry—sheetfed and web. Sheetfed is the most common lithographic process. Gravure sheetfed is also available. In this system, paper is fed through the press, one sheet after another. This is, of course, an automated process, so there are many inventive devices to move the sheet along on its journey through the press. The journey starts off with a puff of air from a blower that is precisely calibrated to separate exactly one sheet from the top of the pile of paper. Then small vacuum feet, which look like tiny suction cups, pick up the sheet. It's important that the sheets start through the press consistently. If they aren't fed straight or if they double up, they'll print poorly and might damage the rubber blanket that's an important part of the image transfer process.

Sets of metal grippers grasp onto the sheet and keep it in place while it travels through the press. Sheets are transferred via gripper-equipped cylinders from one printing unit to the next. The sheets might be printed on one side, dried,

Web Printing Presses

Let it roll

Picture the roll of white paper that's used for cash register receipts. Now imagine a roll of paper that comes up higher than your waist, and you have an idea of what the paper is like that is used for web presses. Instead of single sheets of paper, the web press prints on a long ribbon of paper.

The web press is in the same family as sheetfed systems: It must go through the same steps of feeding, printing, and delivering the paper. The main difference between web and sheetfed presses lies in what happens at the beginning and end of the process. On a web press, the roll of paper is threaded continuously through the machine. When the end of one roll is reached, another is spliced on in a smooth automatic process.

Pages printed on the web are printed in signatures—8, 16, and even 32 pages printed on one big sheet. So as the paper reaches the end of the process, it must also be trimmed and folded.

One of the attractions of the web press is its speed and economy for longer runs. The signatures travel through the system like lightning. You might only see a blur of color as the pages race by. Printing at 25,000 to 80,000 impressions per hour, the web can be three to eight times faster than a sheetfed process.

> **W**eb-fed offset presses can print up to 70,000 newspapers an hour, and are several stories high!

Newspaper printing was the dominant use for the first web presses, which were invented in the mid-1800s in Germany. While web presses are now manufactured in mini and medium widths, those designed for newspapers can be as wide as 108 inches. If you lay four newspaper spreads out side by side, you'll get an idea of how wide a web press can be. By the way, newspaper presses, printing up to 70,000 newspapers an hour, are actually several stories high. For these building-sized presses, as well as with other printing presses these days, the press operators control the job via a console with a cutting-edge computer system that monitors everything from the quality of prints produced to the status of a multitude of press conditions.

The web press is also a popular choice today for printing magazines, brochures, inserts, catalogs, annual reports, packaging, and business forms.

Chapter 3

VITAL SIGNS

The Checkup

Here's where we check out the health and viability of the graphic communications industry. We'll talk, in this next section, about economic markers and industry characteristics. These are important for you to know. Just like a good doctor takes your pulse, temperature, and blood pressure when you go in for a checkup, it's in your best interest to check out the economic viability of the industry.

You're about to choose a path that you may follow over the course of your working life. The information in the next section will help you make sure that your vision for your future is matched and supported by industry outlooks.

Economic Health: A Rosy Picture

If you choose a career in graphic communications, you will be working in the world's largest market for print. With annual sales at $124 billion, the United States produces more print and print-related work than any other country. Within the United States, graphic communications is one of the top ten major manufacturing industries. There are more than 52,000 printing establishments across the country, which means that opportunity is dispersed across the country.

Of those 52,000, small firms are predominant. Eighty percent of all companies in the field have fewer than 20 people on the payroll, while only 3% have more than 100 employees. But the industry is marked by its corporate giants, too. In the 1990s, there has been a flurry of acquisitions and mergers in the printing industry with the result being that most of the big guys have plants and offices in many regions of the country.

More than one million people are employed by the graphic communications industry. Collectively, they pull in more than $36 billion in wages and salaries. Employment is stable. In fact, the good news for those considering this field is that there are more jobs right now for both professional and skilled workers than there are people to fill those jobs. That means that there's a huge ongoing demand for qualified employees. Well-trained and educated workers can expect to earn attractive wages.

Prognosis: Steady Growth

Graphic communications is a growth industry. The demand for printed materials is tied to a number of factors having to do with general economic activity, such as disposable income, the formation of new businesses, money budgeted for advertising, and funding for schools and libraries. With a robust economy and expanding population, business in graphic communications will continue to be brisk.

PRINTING IN THE UNITED STATES

State	Number of Establishments	Number of Employees	$ Sales (In Millions)	State	Number of Establishments	Number of Employees	$ Sales (In Millions)
Alabama	521	7,876	919	Nebraska	422	5,911	698
Alaska	80	1,334	158	Nevada	170	3,539	424
Arizona	684	11,030	1,323	New Hampshire	291	7,565	957
Arkansas	382	7,926	975	New Jersey	2,108	49,425	6,214
California	6,770	89,184	10,366	New Mexico	240	2,302	251
Colorado	845	10,949	1,284	New York	3,759	78,994	9,692
Connecticut	851	20,376	2,567	North Carolina	1,244	24,731	3,017
Delaware	108	2,110	245	North Dakota	140	1,394	145
Dist. of Columbia	135	2,409	280	Ohio	2,467	51,514	6,383
Florida	2,453	32,398	3,762	Oklahoma	631	6,942	787
Georgia	1,136	27,993	3,541	Oregon	685	12,360	1,532
Hawaii	119	1,892	226	Pennsylvania	2,468	59,683	7,536
Idaho	187	2,142	246	Rhode Island	246	4,824	598
Illinois	3,488	79,446	10,001	South Carolina	443	6,794	814
Indiana	1,247	29,806	3,750	South Dakota	183	1,961	216
Iowa	700	13,139	1,612	Tennessee	912	22,583	2,841
Kansas	607	13,488	1,692	Texas	3,250	42,150	4,933
Kentucky	578	15,988	2,040	Utah	323	5,937	718
Louisiana	539	8,920	1,083	Vermont	158	4,069	519
Maine	247	5,993	770	Virginia	852	20,525	2,569
Maryland	806	20,233	2,555	Washington	881	15,724	1,898
Massachusetts	1,480	39,134	4,988	West Virginia	194	2,423	274
Michigan	1,889	33,249	4,029	Wisconsin	1,310	38,562	4,960
Minnesota	1,274	32,705	4,182	Wyoming	83	880	94
Mississippi	271	4,752	567	**Totals**	**52,186**	**1,008,303**	**124,037**
Missouri	1,163	21,459	2,644				
Montana	166	1,580	162				

Courtesy of Printing Industries of America

MARKET SEGMENTS AND PROJECTED GROWTH

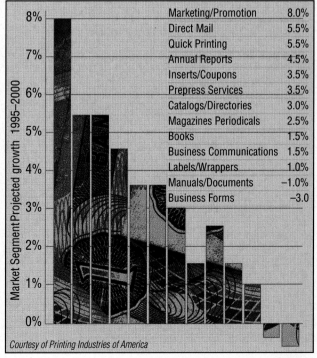

Market Segment	Projected growth 1995–2000
Marketing/Promotion	8.0%
Direct Mail	5.5%
Quick Printing	5.5%
Annual Reports	4.5%
Inserts/Coupons	3.5%
Prepress Services	3.5%
Catalogs/Directories	3.0%
Magazines Periodicals	2.5%
Books	1.5%
Business Communications	1.5%
Labels/Wrappers	1.0%
Manuals/Documents	−1.0%
Business Forms	−3.0

Courtesy of Printing Industries of America

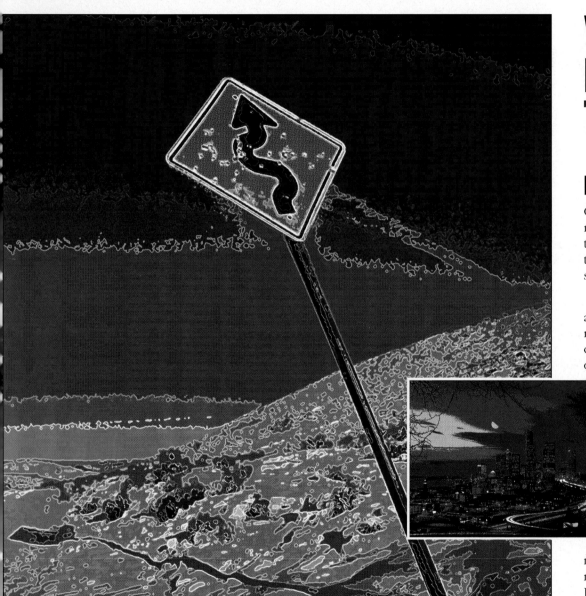

What You Should Know About: The Print Market

Road Trip

Graphic communications can be broken up into smaller segments, each with different challenges, concerns, and opportunities. If the graphic communications industry was a country—the United States, for instance—each one of the market segments would be like one of our individual states.

Each American state has its own personality. Florida has a different feel than South Dakota. Mississippi's character is not the same as New Mexico's or New York's. Despite the contrasts, there's no doubt that each state is part of the overall union.

Market segments work in the same way in the graphic communications industry. Each segment is defined by the goods it produces and the clients it serves. Each segment operates in a slightly different business climate and context. At the same time, there are trends and considerations that affect the industry across all segments.

In this next section, we'll travel across the industry and check out the major market segments. We'll describe the focus of each segment, its economic forecast, and the challenges that make it interesting. Just as driving cross-country can help you to understand our complex nation better, learning about the various market segments should shed some light on the graphic communications industry as a whole. Buckle your seat belts.

General Commercial Printing

The Lowdown

You could say that commercial printers are the primary care doctors of the print world. No, they don't heal the sick. But they are pros who produce a surprising range of products. Just as primary care doctors (or general practitioners, as they were called in the days before managed care) can take care of you whether you have a sore throat or a sprained ankle.

Commercial printers tackle all kinds of large and small printing and graphic communications jobs—from envelopes to CD-ROMS, from brochures to thick catalogs, from invitations to annual reports.

General commercial printing is the number one segment in the graphic communications industry. Here are the stats: There are 40,000 commercial printing establishments in the United States. The workforce numbers around 600,000. The annual revenue is a hefty $74 billion.

Commercial printers work across the spectrum of printing processes—offset lithography, letterpress, gravure, flexography, and screen printing. But offset lithography is where most of the work is for commercial printers. That process accounts for 79% of the business in this market segment. Small and medium-sized commercial printing companies serve clients who are close at hand—in their local area or the surrounding region. Larger commercial printers also produce work for national and international accounts. It's not uncommon, for instance, for a corporation in Massachusetts to send its work to a printer in Texas, if that printer is the one who will best meet its needs. Satellite transmissions, overnight delivery services, the Internet, and the fax have made it increasingly feasible for large printers to work with distant clients.

The Buzz

There's a lot of good news for general commercial printers these days. The demand for printed products is tied to the general economic activity. With a current economy that is robust, commercial printers who are responsive to their customers' needs can expect to do a healthy business. The population in the United States will have increased by 12 million between 1993 and 1998. Two million new businesses will have started up over roughly that same period. This all bodes well for the commercial printer who should see sales grow at an annual rate of 4.5–6%.

On the Horizon

Ink on paper—the traditional product of the printing industry—will not go the way of the dinosaur. In fact, since we are in an information-driven society, the need for "ink on paper" will continue to grow.

At the same time, the means through which we get our information are rapidly changing as the 21st century begins. The graphic communications industry is reshaping itself in response. Many experts believe that printers will soon consider themselves to be in the "imaging" or communications industry rather than the printing business. The star that printers will hitch themselves to will be digital in nature. Members of the graphic communications industry will be experts in the creation and delivery of electronic images that can be output as ink on paper. But those images may also be configured as electronic and digital products such as CD-ROMs, electronic databases, the World Wide Web, the Internet, and interactive software. As graphic communicators, printers will be on the cutting edge.

Newspaper Printing

The Lowdown

Newspaper printing is the second largest market segment of the graphic communications industry. It employs 478,000 people across the United Statess. According to recent figures, annual revenue is $41 billion.

Daily newspapers, many of which also print a thicker and more expensive Sunday issue, have the highest circulation (number of copies printed and sold). There are more weekly newspapers in existence than dailies—almost five times as many, as a matter of fact. But weekly papers have a much lower circulation figure. The two most common types of weekly papers are community newspapers and alternative newspapers. A community newspaper focuses on a small, well-defined populace, such as the residents of one borough or neighborhood. More community newspapers are being founded in suburban areas as the population shifts further from the cities. Alternative papers often report on news stories that they feel aren't being covered in the traditional city dailies.

Newspapers are also distinguished by their form. A gatefold paper is one that is divided into individual sections such as news, sports, business, and life-style sections. Tabloids are printed as one long, thick section, in the same way that a book or magazine is.

Newspapers are printed using one of three printing processes: web letterpress, flexography, or web offset lithography. Newspapers are printed on a relatively inexpensive grade of paper called newsprint. The United States, by the way, consumes over one-third of the world's supply of newsprint paper.

The Buzz

Readership of newspapers is on the decline. Surveys indicate that each succeeding generation reads newspapers less than did their parents. But while circulation is stagnant or dropping, circulation revenue has risen. Newspapers still turn a profit. Economists predict a stable 1–2% annual growth rate for this market.

Newspapers make most of their profit through advertising revenue. They suffered greatly at the beginning of this decade when the economic picture was so gloomy that advertisers drastically cut their budgets. Although levels of advertising have risen as the economy has become more robust, advertisers are still working with tighter budgets and are therefore more selective about how to best reach consumers.

Newspapers have responded by creating special sections, for example a "Wheels" section to pull in readers especially interested in automobiles, or a large pull-out bridal section for those planning weddings. These special sections are appealing to certain advertisers because they know they will reach the consumers who will be interested in their products or services. Zoned editions are another nontraditional approach. These are sections of the paper targeted for people who live in a certain geographical area. Zoned sections are also popular with advertisers and help newspapers compete for dollars with direct mail advertising.

On the Horizon

Many newspapers are redefining themselves as providers of information products in a variety of formats, including electronic. Newspapers were among the earliest to jump on the World Wide Web bandwagon and put the daily news on-line. Look for them to continue to be leaders in offering Internet and on-line services to reach new readers and to create value-added products for subscribers. As newspapers become even more sophisticated in competing with other types of media for advertising dollars, they will move even further into the development of database marketing and other electronic information services.

Courtesy Gannett Company

Book Printing

The Lowdown

With roots that go back to Gutenberg's Bible in the mid-15th century, book printing is the great-great-great-great-great-great grandfather of all of the graphic communications market segments. And despite the ancient ties, books are not in any danger of becoming outmoded or old-fashioned. An average of 50,000 titles are published each year in the United States. Seventy million adults say that they buy books on a regular basis. Future market trends suggest anywhere from a 2% to a 4.7% annual increase in total dollar volume in the coming years.

Book printing is a $5.9 billion annual business, employing 49,000 workers at 600 establishments. More than 25% of published books fall into the trade category—the industry buzzword for general interest books such as mysteries, biographies, and how-to books. Another quarter of the market is dominated by the production of textbooks for elementary, high school, and college. Technical, scientific, and professional books account for a 17% piece of the pie. Mass-market paperbacks check in at 7%. That leaves a little less than one-fourth of the market for a hodgepodge of books, including reference books, university press publications, religious books, and books produced for the book-club and mail-order business.

While books can certainly be printed using the letterpress method, most printers today find it economically wise to go the lithography route.

The Buzz

Bookstores—especially the superstore with its cozy ambiance of cappuccino, jazz trios, and, oh yes, books—are in these days. They've been one of the reasons behind a spurt in consumer demand for books. Books in all categories are seeing an increase in sales. The superstore, with its huge inventory, has helped firm up the market for books that have a significant demand but a more narrowly defined audience than those on the bestseller list.

Books do battle for the consumer's leisure budget with a variety of other information and entertainment products and services—cable television, VCRs, video games, and other multimedia products. And they are competing successfully. Seven percent is the expected annual increase in total volume of book sales over the next few years; the profit stream looks to be steady. The advent—and adoption—over the last ten years of desktop publishing systems that can digitize text and images has meant significant savings in the cost of preparing a book for publication.

On the Horizon

Books are by no means eating the dust of the late 20th-century sprint toward electronic publishing. Electronic products and services are putting an exhilarating spin on a book publisher's traditional offerings. And book printers are right in the thick of the challenge. Printers are the right arm of the publisher. As the market is expanding, so are the capabilities of the printer. Historically, printers have taken the images and text for a book and used their expertise to prepare and output that material onto paper. Now printers are extending their craftsmanship to electronic realms. As they work with the digitized information that can be printed as a book, they might also prepare that same information for life as a CD-ROM, an interactive software product, or for the Internet and the Web.

Digital technology is not only transforming the final product. It is having a tremendous impact on the front end of the process as well—an impact that is allowing the printer to be an even better partner to the publisher. With conventional printing processes, efficiencies of scale meant that the more books printed per run, the lower the cost per volume. This set up an economy that often resulted in publishers carrying huge inventories that were not always profitable. On-demand printing, also known as just-in-time printing, allows books to be printed economically in short runs. Printers produce books in response to consumer demand; publishers avoid the financial pitfalls of overordering; everyone is happy. On-demand printing is the largest growth area for book printers today.

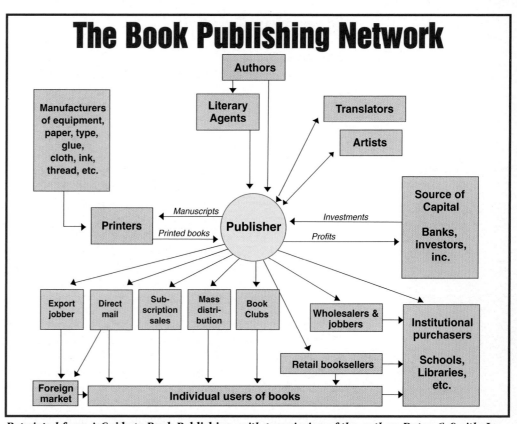

The Book Publishing Network

Reprinted from **A Guide to Book Publishing,** *with permission of the author, Datus C. Smith, Jr.*

Courtesy IDG Books Worldwide, Inc.

Magazine Printing

The Lowdown

Magazines continue to be popular and slick vehicles for information and entertainment. Recent figures place the number of American magazines at about 11,000. In the United States, 123,000 people work in magazine printing at 312 plants. (Periodicals are published in just about every state in the country.) Annual sales in magazine printing register at $26.4 billion, putting it in the solid middle of the graphic communication industry's market segments. Women's magazines, newsweeklies like *Time* and *Newsweek,* business magazines, and general interest magazines such as *Reader's Digest* and *National Geographic* pull in the most advertising revenue, followed by sports, Sunday feature, entertainment, home and house improvement, travel, and parenting magazines.

Magazine publishing has always been a volatile enterprise. Over one-half of magazines fold before they celebrate their first anniversary. (One reason for the high failure rate: It takes relatively little capital to bring a new magazine to market. Fledgling publishers jump in with a good idea—and a too-sketchy business plan.) In the late 1980s and early 1990s, 900 new magazines plunged in. Over the same time period, 760 bit the dust.

Magazines are printed on both web and sheetfed presses using offset lithography, letterpress, and gravure. Gravure has long been the choice for large consumer magazines with circulation figures in the millions. Now with electronic prepress and direct-digital platemaking becoming the norm, the start-up costs for gravure are dropping. Some experts expect to see more magazines make the shift to gravure.

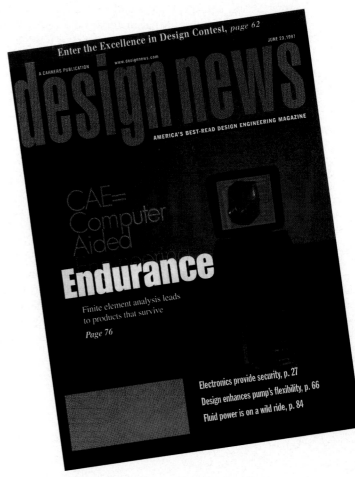

Courtesy Cahners Business Information

The Buzz

The rise and fall of magazine readership is affected by competition from other media (direct mail and catalogs especially) as well as by economic conditions and changing production technology. Production expenses and postal rates continue to rise. The market has entered into a stable, mature phase, following a tremendous period of sustained growth in the 1980s. As with newspapers, magazine publishers are creating nar-  rowly defined magazines geared to smaller, targeted audiences, such as dirt-bike enthusiasts or owners of Siamese cats as opposed to the more general topics of outdoor sports or pets. Prospects look good for the magazine market to continue to grow at a 3–5% level.

On the Horizon

The goal of advertisers is, as always, to reach the consumers who are most likely to be interested in their product. Magazines continue to push the envelope in responding to that need—and they must in order to stay viable. Selective binding techniques, which are complex software systems, make it possible to customize publications by inserting selective advertising and editorial content targeted for readers with special interests or of certain geographical regions. As are newspapers, forward-thinking magazine publishers see themselves as providers of information services, which will increasingly and rapidly include CD-ROM, the Internet, World Wide Web, and electronic database services.

Courtesy **Wired** *Magazine*

Quick Printing

The Lowdown

Quick print shops are the convenience stores of the graphic communications industry. This is a market niche based on customer service. Quick printing sprung to life in the 1970s and 1980s and grew at a fast and furious rate. Quick print houses are generally retail shops located in high traffic areas that attract a lot of shoppers. Traditionally, they have served walk-in clients with short-run jobs, producing high-quality work in as short a time as possible. As the whole industry moves toward shorter runs, quick printers are now serving a wider range of clients, particularly because they've been ahead of the curve electron-ically. Recent figures show 40,000 quick printing businesses employing 396,000 workers. Annual sales for the industry are $20.9 billion.

The Buzz

Forecasts indicate that the quickprint segment will grow at an annual rate of 5.5%. The customer base for quick printers tends to be drawn from small enterprises such as retail shops, real estate offices, architectural firms, law firms, nonprofit groups, as well as individuals with a one-time need for printing services.

On the Horizon

Competition has been stirring as small commercial printers also equip themselves for the fast turn-around work that is the traditional stronghold of quick printers. At the same time, many quick printers are positioning themselves on the vanguard of electronic printing technologies, offering new value-added services, such as electronic archiving, database publishing, and computer rental, to their customers. Expect quick printers to keep pace with the changing nature of the graphic communications industry.

Financial Printing

The Lowdown

Financial printing is one of the narrowly defined, highly specialized market niches in the graphic communications industry. Financial printers provide printing services to companies whose stock is publicly traded. Why is this a special niche, you might ask? How do these printing services differ from the run-of-the-mill daily business needs of small and large companies across the country? Well, the federal government, through the Securities and Exchange Commission (SEC), tries to keep a pretty tight rein on the stock market. One of the ways it accomplishes this is by regulating how information about stocks and securities is provided and released to the public. Financial printers not only know the printing process inside out, but they blend that knowledge with expertise about government-mandated forms, pamphlets, and securities prospectuses—the preliminary statements that describe a company to prospective investors. The SEC dictates hundreds of minute details about these publications, everything from when they must be published to the kind of paper and the size of the print that must be used.

The process of producing these kinds of documents is a complicated one. And it's made even more touchy by the fact that the financial printer is dealing with sensitive, highly confidential financial information. In fact, the successful financial printer tackles the job as a supportive partner to the company. The financial printer may work with a business for the first time when the company is making its Initial Public Offering (IPO, in Wall Street lingo). Ultimately, long-term relationships characterize this segment of the graphic communications industry. In addition to the IPO documents, financial printers may help their clients to produce documents for secondary stock offerings as well as mergers and acquisitions. In the dog-eat-dog world of the stock market, it is easy to see how a financial printer who is rock-solid on government disclosure regulations is a huge asset to its clients.

By the way, financial printing is one of the few market segments in the graphic communications industry to be associated primarily with one particular area. Most of the financial printing business is established in New York City.

The Buzz

The fortune of financial printers will always follow the rise and fall of the stock exchange. In 1996, financial printers rode high on the crest of Wall Street's bull market. IPOs were heavy. In the first nine months of 1996 alone, sales revenues from the printing of prospectuses were more than $100 million. The corporate world bustled with major mergers and restructuring. The result was a record year for financial printers.

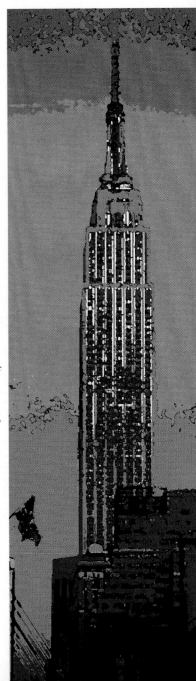

On the Horizon

Electronic submission of information is making inroads into the way that business is done in the financial printing world. An electronic SEC filing system called EDGAR (Electronic Data Gathering Analysis and Retrieval) became fully operational in 1996. In addition, the World Wide Web is ripe with opportunity for the quick distribution of information crucial to the lightning pace of financial markets. But perhaps even more so in financial printing than in any other area of graphic communications, printers are taking a leading role in helping their customers to see what electronic publishing can mean for their business. Savvy financial printers understand that businesses will always need hard copies of their financial documents. But in addition, these specialized printers will now bring their expertise to the electronic submission of sensitive financial information as well as to the use of the World Wide Web.

WHAT YOU SHOULD KNOW ABOUT: HISTORY

This Is a History That Will Make You Proud

Digital imaging. Electronic scanning. Direct-to-plate printing. Graphic communications is an exciting place to be as the 21st century nears—precisely because it is a 21st-century industry. Change is happening at a fast and furious rate, and it is breathing new life into this long-established trade. Talk to anyone in the business these days, and you will be talking to someone who is charged up. Press operators, prepress specialists, sales people, binding supervisors, company owners—they're all spinning with ideas about how to tweak and customize the new technologies and processes.

The modern-day print shop, though, would be unrecognizable to Ts'ai Lun, who invented paper in the beginning of the 2nd century in China, or even to Johannes Gutenberg, who went deeply into debt in the middle of the 15th century to develop a workable system of printing in Germany. Still, contemporary printing sits on the shoulders of the inventions and discoveries of ancient Imperial China and the European Middle Ages. These were inventions so powerful they altered the course of civilization.

First, Paper

The only constant of the last half of the 20th century, as the popular saying goes, is change.

Given the pace of the 20th century, it might be a little hard to imagine the long, slow development—over more than 1,500 years—that it took to get all the pieces in place in order for printing to be invented.

The first piece of this evolution lies in the development of paper. Time was still running on BC clocks back when the Greeks and Romans began to experiment with the papyrus plant that grew in the marshes of the Nile River. They learned that by pressing the plant's spongy tissue they could make a material with a surface smooth enough to be written on. Later, parchment made from the skins of cattle, sheep, and goats would become the writing surface of choice. Papermaking, one of the necessary prerequisites for "artificial writing," as printing was first called, would not be established in Europe until the 14th century.

It was a different story in China where paper was invented by Ts'ai Lun at the start of the 2nd century. The secret of papermaking passed to the Arab world in the middle of the 8th century, probably by Chinese soldiers that had been taken prisoner. Soon paper mills were cooking up pulp and turning it into paper in Baghdad, and later in Arab-controlled Spain. But not until the 12th century was paper traded in Italy and France. And it was another two centuries before it was manufactured in Europe and made widely available.

One Book at a Time

Imagine how small the world was when knowledge and information could only be shared by books hand-copied arduously, painstakingly, one by one by one. Imagine how long it would take for discoveries to be communicated, for advancements to be understood. The wider-spread manufacture of paper meant that a book could finally be made more cheaply than those using parchment or vellum. But it did nothing to reduce the amount of time it took one scribe to produce one book.

The progress of civilization hinged on the ability to reproduce books quickly and efficiently.

Central Casting

Enter Johannes Gutenberg, now of Gutenberg Bible fame. By the time Gutenberg came on the scene, the idea of printing was already established. Trouble is, it was done by carving wooden blocks in the shape of illustrations or alphabet letters. China can claim the world's first known printed book—*Diamond Sutra*, printed in 868 with wood block. The wooden blocks were inked, and paper was pressed against them to create an image. If you've ever taken an art class, you've probably taken a stab at making your own wood-block print. Wood-block printing can be beautiful and effective. But it's not a system that works for mass production. For one thing, the wood wears out easily. For another, a whole page is carved onto one block. If a mistake is made or a change desired, the entire block has to be thrown out and a new one arduously created.

The first thing Gutenberg did was carve out punches for the entire set of capital and small letters as well as punctuation marks like commas and periods. On these punches, the characters were set in relief—above the surface. (Picture the keys of a typewriter.) The next step would be to use the punches to create a matrix for each character. A matrix is a mold that can be used over and over again. Replicas of each character could then be cast by pouring molten lead into the matrix.

> *G*utenberg knew that books were in high demand. He knew that whoever figured out a way to reproduce them could stand to earn a fortune.

The magnificence of Gutenberg's invention had to do with the three elements—punch, matrix, and type—working together as a system. As opposed to wood-block printing, this movable metal type was durable and could be assembled as necessary. Also, thousands of identical pieces of type could be cast. This was an important consideration. Setting the type for a single page required many characters. To compose an entire book, thousands would be necessary.

There were other benefits to Gutenberg's system. Hundreds of copies could be made—and with great speed compared to hand copying. Each copy would be identical to the first. In addition, accuracy could be greatly improved. It would now be possible to edit, proof, and correct the pages of text. And the metal type pieces could be reused later in the printing of an entirely different book.

Gutenberg is often called the inventor of the printing press. But his invention of metal movable type was the truly revolutionary achievement. The wooden press Gutenberg developed was adapted from the mechanism long used to press grapes or cheese—which is how the printing device got its name. A similar contraption would have been used in times earlier than Gutenberg's for wood-block printing as well.

This wooden screw-and-lever press worked by lowering a heavy plate called a platen against a typeform that is held horizontally in the waist-high bed of the press to make an inked impression on a sheet of paper. Gutenberg's press could deliver 20 printed sheets in one hour—laborious in terms of today's standards, lightning fast in comparison to the alternatives of the day. Gutenberg's system of printing worked so well that, with only small changes along the way, it stood for three centuries before being replaced by other methods of printing.

A Playwright's Revenge

Alois Senefelder

Toward the end of the 18th century, a determined young playwright, Alois Senefelder, frustrated because he hadn't been able to get his plays published, decided to take matters into his own hands. He would print and distribute his plays himself. By now, the state of the art in printing included a method known as intaglio, which included engraving and etching images and text onto copper plates to be printed.

But copper was expensive. So Senefelder began to experiment. Limestone slate was abundant in Bavaria where he lived, and he found a way to make plates with this material. At first, he used acid to etch a slightly raised image onto the limestone surface. But this didn't work entirely to his satisfaction. It was hard to keep the ink away from the area around the image. This problem turned out to be the key, though. It led him to realize it wasn't necessary for the printed surface to be raised. Using a greasy kind of pencil he made from wax, soap, and lampblack, he began drawing right onto the limestone. The limestone attracted water, but rejected the ink, which was made with an oil base. On the other hand, the part of the stone where Senefelder drew with the greasy pencil rejected water

and attracted the ink. Senefelder could prepare the limestone plate using these properties of water and oil so that the stone accepted ink where he wanted to print and kept the ink away from the nonimage areas. What he had discovered was a printing process based on chemical rather than mechanical properties. Legend has it that the first page Senefelder printed using this method was not for one of his plays after all, but a laundry list for his mother, who was furious at him for having used up all of the paper in the house for his experiments. Senefelder's method became known as lithography, and it went on to transform the landscape of the printing trade.

A Reversal of Fortune

The lithography that Senefelder invented was a direct process: what was printed was a mirror image of the type or illustration. This meant that in order to produce a page of text, for instance, that was right-reading, the image on the lithography plate had to be created in reverse.

But a little more than one hundred years after Senefelder invented lithography (which, by the way, means writing by stone), an American printer named Ira Rubel transformed lithography—by accident. By this time, rotary presses, which run with impression cylinders rather than flat plates, had come into favor. Litho stones had always been clumsy and awkward to handle. Now thin metal plates were being manufactured to take the place of the stones. The metal, which could be prepared to reject water and attract ink in the same way as the stones, was also flexible enough to be wrapped around a cylinder.

A paper-feed stoppage occurred one day in Rubel's shop. The mechanized press shut down, but not before an image happened to be transferred from the image plate cylinder of the rotary press to the rubber blanket that cushioned the impression cylinder.

Rubel had his wits about him that day. He noticed that this rubber blanket itself was able to transfer the image. Not only that, but it produced a sharper image. And the big bonus was that two negatives make a positive. By transferring the image twice—from a plate to the rubber blanket to the paper—the image no longer had to be printed from its reverse.

Rubel's discovery led to the development of the three-cylinder printing press. (The three cylinders are the plate, blanket, and impression cylinders.) The process that used this three-cylinder system became known as offset lithography. Today, this method is so widely used that most lithography is simply called offset.

You Say You Want a Revolution?

If you had a nickel for every time someone in the printing industry in the last twenty years has announced a change as being the most revolutionary since Gutenberg, you'd be wealthy. Exaggerations aside, it is true that the recent history of printing has been marked by a remarkable series of transformations.

To give you an idea of how quickly and profoundly change has come about, a 1978 graphic communications technology report mentioned microprocessors—and was quick to explain what they were. Not everyone would have known.

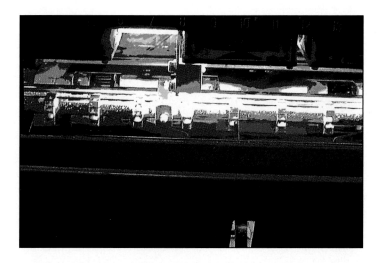

Speaking of desktop publishing—here is another concept that has transformed the graphic communications industry in just a little more than ten years time. Rather than hand-assembling text and graphics, desktop publishing systems work with multitasking computer software to integrate these two very different procedures electronically. Desktop publishing was first associated with the Macintosh, although it was eventually available on other systems. It has blurred the traditional responsibilities of graphic designers and printers and opened up many new possibilities.

Digital computer-controlled printing equipment is state-of-the-art technology.

This was around the time that early electronic scanners were first being introduced into the prepress area of sophisticated print shops. (Digital electronic scanners can take a photograph or drawing and convert it into a digital image for printing plates, CD-ROMs, or the World Wide Web.) By 1987, a mere nine years later, 90% of all color separations in the world were made using electronic scanners. With a scanner, a color separation, which would take about two hours to produce using old photographic methods, could be completed in twenty minutes. Scanning technology has proliferated—both at the high-resolution end necessary for top-quality printing as well as lower-resolution systems suitable for a variety of printing needs. In fact today, because of desktop publishing, you wouldn't be any more surprised to see a desktop scanner in an office than you would a coffee maker. (Of course, the desktop scanner is not the same quality as the scanner in a print shop.) The big trend in electronic scanning technology for printers now is the addition of artificial intelligence capabilities to diagnose and adjust the quality of a color scan.

Within the short span of twenty years, every facet of printing has come under the influence of the computer and microprocessor. Digital computer-controlled printing equipment is state-of-the-art technology. The landscape of the trade has been redrawn.

History is being made.

THE CRYSTAL BALL
Does Print Have a Future?

Well, you don't really need a crystal ball to see that print does, indeed, have a future—quite a promising one, for that matter.

In the first place, experts say that the volume of printed information doubles every five years. That fact alone should convince you that folks in the graphic communications industry are going to have more than enough work to keep them busy. (And don't forget—that translates into plenty of jobs for newcomers to the field.)

The U.S. economy is information-driven. And print will retain its role as the primary vehicle for information, even as the electronic transmission of information increases. The print industry plays a big role in packaging, for instance. Packaging is more important than ever for catching the eyes of consumers hurrying through the store as well as for providing important information about the product. Then there are books: All the studies show that people are not about to curl up with their monitor instead of a good book. And as far as the "paperless" office that's been predicted—well, hard copies of important documents are not going the way of the dinosaur any time soon. Look for electronic and traditional ink-on-paper media to exist side by side for a long time.

And that's especially good news. You see, you could think about the printing industry as being in the business of serving information. Printers aren't cooking up the information, but they're the ones who get it to the table while it's still hot—whether that table is a paper table or electronic. Traditional print will increase over the next five years—and so will the use of electronic media. For savvy printers, this is a win-win situation.

Increasingly, CD-ROMs, the Internet, World Wide Web, interactive CDs, and electronic print-on-demand services are cutting inroads into the printing industry. Forward-thinking printers are going to capture that business.

For someone entering the field, it means that both traditional and alternative media will proliferate. And no matter what kind of job in the graphic communications industry interests you, you will be involved with highly advanced technologies at a very sophisticated, challenging, and interesting level.

So how will emerging media and digital technology transform the industry? What will the printing industry look like down the road?

First of all, the nature of the role of printer is changing. Technology as well as economic changes are driving the transformation of the printing industry into the visual communications industry. Most successful printing companies are beginning to think of their product in terms of visual imaging and communications. Those who provide prepress services especially see themselves as being in an imaging business that can be applied to a wide range of media, both traditional and alternative. New products and services will focus on the integration of data and multimedia services.

A career in graphic communications, as we turn the bend toward the 21st century, means having one foot planted firmly in a time-honored tradition, the other stepping of into a new land. In this section, we'll take a look at some of the features of that new land.

The Move to Market-Driven: We're Not in Kansas Anymore

A dramatic change in personality—that's what the graphic communications industry has undergone in recent years. Traditionally, printers have seen themselves as highly skilled craftspeople whose job it was to produce a certain product. But as intelligent computer systems and digital technology have become a pervasive feature of the printing world, and as consumers become more comfortable with the notion of the global marketplace, the printed product has come to be considered a commodity.

What does that mean, and what does it have to do with you? Well, first let's define commodity. When a product becomes viewed as a commodity, it means that the public believes it can count on any number of suppliers to provide what it needs. A translation: I can go to any printer, and have my job produced to my satisfaction and at a reasonable cost. It's sort of the way you know you can find someone who makes custom tee-shirts or pierces ears in any mall in the United States.

In this kind of market, then, the question is: "What makes a client choose one printer over another?"

Lower prices, quick turnaround, you might answer. And you wouldn't be wrong. Rapid service and the best solution for the least amount of money

will always be important considerations for a client. But it's not as simple as that. The industry has become market-driven now, rather than manufacturing-driven. This shift in business perspective affects everyone from the CEO or owner down to an assistant production worker.

Here's how: Printers all over the country are becoming aware that they need to see themselves as being in the business of helping their clients to be successful. How can they do this? By understanding and meeting their clients' communication needs. An important element of this mission will continue to be the production of print. But increasingly, printers must anticipate technological trends and understand their various clients' businesses well enough to lead the way on how new media might serve their needs. Rather than be a provider of a product, the graphic communications worker becomes a provider of solutions—both print and electronic.

Brave New (Binary) World

Digital is fun, no doubt about it. There's a lot of enthusiasm, vigor, and interest for figuring out how digital processes and technologies can be applied throughout the print shop. But leading-edge technology is also shifting the identity of graphic communications from a craft-based manufacturing industry to an electronic-based service industry. This section will discuss two up-and-coming digital technologies that are infiltrating the industry: computer-to-plate (CTP) and digital photography.

Computer-to-Plate (CTP)

Picture a typical page in a magazine. You're used to seeing photographs, illustrations, and words routinely appear on the same page. Yet in a conventional printing process, text is prepared for printing one way; photographs and line drawings another. Someone has to bring all of these elements together, and that is part of the work that you will hear referred to as prepress. There are many steps involved in the conventional prepress process. One of the steps involves assembling the page elements by hand. Text and images are placed together according to the layout created by a graphic designer, resulting in a composite called a mechanical or pasteup. In another part of the process, the mechanical is photographed with a special graphic arts camera and a negative or positive piece of film is made. That piece of film is used to expose a photosensitive plate that will be used for printing. Finally, the page is ready for the printing press.

As computers have made dramatic inroads into the prepress area, many of the time-consuming aspects of hand-preparing materials for printing have been replaced with electronic processes. With desktop publishing, for instance, images can be scanned and combined electronically with the text. That electronically-assembled page is then output from an imagesetter to film. The process from this point on is the same as the conventional printing process.

This direct-to-film process that is the hallmark of desktop publishing, by the way, is now pretty much the way things are done in print shops.

Computer-to-plate, or CTP, pushes the digital process one step further, bypassing the film stage of production. With CTP, digital data is recorded directly from the electronically assembled page onto a special printing plate, using a large-format laser imager rather than a graphic arts camera.

There are lots of benefits to CTP. The quality of the images on the plate are improved. In order to be printed, photographs, for instance, have to be translated into a series of tiny dots—similar to television's square "pixels" that carry the image on your screen. The laser-exposed dots of CTP are extremely crisp and clean and maintain their crispness longer during the pressrun, resulting in high quality printed images. And CTP is relatively fast.

CTP is becoming widely adopted. Some printers are using CTP exclusively; many others use CTP technology alongside more conventional platemaking efforts. In 1995, 6% of all printers polled had introduced CTP into their facilities. That number was expected to rise to 33% in 1997. Look for this process to be a direct hit.

Digital Photography

Digital photography is part of the ever-accelerating trend to work with images in digitized form. With digital photography it's not necessary to go through the intermediate step of scanning a photographic print so that it can be placed electronically in a page layout. Instead, the photograph is recorded in digital form in the first place.

A digital camera is cousin to the video camcorder. Like a camcorder, it uses photosensitive CCDs (charge-coupled devices)—electronic sensors that record the image. It does this by converting light into electrical impulses that can be read by a computer. A photographer can view this digital image immediately on a monitor. In fact, one of the attractions of this technology is that there is no downtime while an image is being scanned or film is processed. Once captured, the image is ready to be used electronically—for printing or CD-ROM purposes as well as for publishing on the Internet or World Wide Web.

There are many for whom digital photography promises a competitive edge. Large retailers, who rely on catalogs and circulars to advertise their products, for instance, were the earliest users of digital photography. Although digital cameras can be more than ten times as expensive as their conventional counterparts at this point in their development, a retail business whose print runs number in the millions can offset the expense of the equipment with big savings on film and processing costs. Newspapers have also been quick to incorporate digital cameras into their operation. In this case, one of the selling points is their effectiveness in showing the latest breaking news from anywhere in the world. Digital photographs can be recorded, sent by modem or satellite to the newspaper, and placed directly into the newspaper layout in a matter of minutes.

From a quality point of view, high-resolution digital cameras can offer a stunning level of detail. Greater color fidelity and control is possible than with conventional silver-based photography. Digital photography is also a more environmentally friendly process. Since it is filmless, the toxic chemicals that are a part of film processing don't enter into the picture.

As the digital camera moves more and more into the mainstream, its price will continue to drop at the same time that quality will improve. At present, high-resolution studio cameras suitable for shooting still scenes cost anywhere from $9,500 to $36,000. For outside the studio, hand-held digital cameras—traditional SLRs with digital backs—run between $10,000 and $28,000, although some digital cameras now available for limited purposes are as inexpensive as $350.

The market for digital cameras grows as steadily as the clamor for digital images.

Emerging Media: Can You Say "Repurpose?"

Perhaps to an even greater extent than most industries, emerging electronic technologies—the Internet, World Wide Web, and CD-ROM—are both piquing and challenging the interests of graphic communications. The truth is, though, that the Internet and the World Wide Web are teenagers. They generate a ton of energy, but nobody knows for sure yet what they're going to be when they grow up.

That doesn't make the 'Net, Web, or CD-ROM any less critical to the future of the graphic communications industry. It does make it interesting, however, to try to predict what the coming years will hold and how these new media will shape the future. One thing is clear: these technologies are going to relandscape the business.

The Internet has been around since the late 1960s, when the Department of Defense (DOD) decided it would be a good idea to create a computer network to link military, government, and university sites. What they were going for was a communications system that was fail-safe. The DOD reasoned that if the pathways of this network were diffused rather than centralized, the system could withstand assault. Thus the Internet was born.

But the information superhighway that has dazzled us in the 1990s with its communication potential and speed was used more like an old two-lane blacktop road back in the late '60s. It was next to impossible for anyone but the most expert computer users to find their way around to access information.

Of course that's all changed. In the past few years, the development of web browsers like Internet Explorer and Netscape and the availability of simple page development software has led to the intense commercialization of the Internet. The expectation of immediate and individual access is reshaping the way that business takes place. At times it seems as if corporate America now feels pressured to gather information at a pace approaching star speed. For sure, interactive digital media is the fastest growing of all the segments in the communications industry. CD-ROM and DVD (digital versatile disk) technologies, with their ability to record huge amounts of data, graphics, and video and audio information, are serving up multimedia products for the computer.

So there's money to be made. But what does this have to do with the graphic communications industry? How are these emerging media related to printing?

As with all of industry, printers are finding that the Internet and Web offer new ways for them to interact with clients. Through its presence on the Web, a printing company can introduce itself to potential customers, present its services, respond to email queries, take in bids on a job, and provide existing clients with job-related specs as well as up-to-the-minute instructions for the digital submission of a print job. Many printers use the Internet as a way of receiving electronic materials for printing from distant clients.

The most startling effect that these new media will have on the graphic communications industry is the very products and services that printers will offer. Forward-thinking printers already understand that the same pages that are being electronically prepared for ink-on-paper applications can

Faster Than a Speeding Train— It's a Bird. It's a Plane. It's...

On-demand printing

Okay, maybe Superman could beat it. But as printing processes go, this one is the track star of the graphic communications industry. And the all-around athlete, too.

First and foremost, on-demand printing is the ability to print a job, say a document, book, manual, or brochure, quickly and as needed. For instance, a printer with on-demand capabilities might receive an order for 300 perfect-bound books at 9:00 a.m. and by noon the books are printed, bound, and sitting in neat stacks waiting to be shipped out.

An outgrowth of desktop publishing, on-demand printing is an electronic process through and through. The printing job moves directly from computer to printing press, without the intermediate step of printing plates.

After the initial prepress work has been completed, the whole document may be archived electronically until the client needs to have it produced. The sheer speed of on-demand printing is a terrific advantage, especially when time is more important than money. Not that money isn't important. In fact, another attraction of on-demand printing is the lower cost associated with start-up. Smaller runs can be produced economically, reducing the need for a publisher to tie up money in a huge inventory. Also, because the document is stored electronically, it's easy enough to customize the print run with pages or information that varies. For instance, one version of the document might be created for a market in the Southwest, while a slightly different edition is printed for the New England area.

Forecast: Expect on-demand printing to continue to be the hot new printing technology. By the year 2000, experts predict this will be a $21 billion market, commanding 15% of the total print market and growing at a rate of nearly 15% annually.

be—and here is the big industry buzzword—repurposed for applications to other electronic media.

The digital storage of information in electronic archives —complicated and extensive databases, for instance—is also seen as a transforming business opportunity. Printers on the cutting edge believe electronic archiving to be a natural extension of their services, as they come to see themselves as information brokers as well as print experts.

The bottom line: now is the time to become one of the pioneers in the graphic communications industry—creating, defining, and mastering a new land of electronic possibility.

Chapter 7

Prepress

CAREER CLOSE-UPS

Nice Work—And You Can Get It!

So graphic communications is beginning to sound like an interesting field to you. But you still have lots of unanswered questions: What exactly would I be doing? What kinds of jobs are available?

Opportunities in graphic communications can be technical or production-oriented as well as of a professional or administrative nature. On the production side, work is usually broken down into three areas: prepress, press, and finishing.

In this section of the book, we will take a look at some of the specific occupations within the industry. We'll describe how those roles fit into the overall graphic communications process. And we'll give you the inside scoop on the kind of background, skills, and training those roles require.

CAREER CLOSE-UPS: Technical Roles— Prepress

The First Leg

Prepress is where the production journey begins for a printed piece. These days, most prepress work is done electronically, and technological advances continue to rapidly reshape the way that prepress happens.

In terms of career opportunities, the newer, computer-oriented imaging operations will provide tremendous opportunities for those possessing expertise in electronic imaging skills. Computer literacy is a must.

The journey of a project through the prepress department often begins with preflighting, where the disks supplied by the customer are examined for potential problems that might affect how the job will print. If there are problems, a file repair technician will work on remedying them once the customer has okayed the repairs. The scanner operator scans photographs and illustrations, converting them electronically into high-resolution, digital images. At the customer's request, these images may be manipulated electronically to produce the most desirable results. The digital files are then integrated into the page layout.

An output technician might be responsible for several parts of the next phase. Photographic negatives of each page must be electronically assembled, or imposed, in a very precise manner with other pages onto what is called a flat. At this point, page proofs are created. These proofs represent what the final printed product will look like. The page proofs are presented to the customer for approval.

When the proofs have been approved, the platemaker takes the flat and creates the printing plates which will be shipped off to the pressroom for printing. A prepress supervisor or manager oversees the workflow and policies of the prepress department and coordinates work with the managers of the other departments.

Traditionally, the craftspeople in a prepress department had clearly defined roles. If you were a typesetter, a stripper, or a photoengraver, for instance, that would be the only work you did. In today's new electronic prepress environment, the roles tend to be blurred. One person may be responsible for several different facets of production. Some believe that, in technological terms, the prepress, or imaging, department is one of the most exciting places in a graphic communications shop. Certainly it is the area that is undergoing the greatest change.

Preflight Technician: All Systems Go

In Search Of

Individual who likes working with computers and software applications. Pays attention to detail. Likes to go looking for trouble.

Check it out

The preflight technician is first and foremost a trouble-shooter. Before an airplane takes off, standard operating procedure has the pilot run through a checklist to make sure everything is in order. Mid-air is not where you want to

discover a faulty fuel gauge, for instance. It's the same deal in the prepress department. You don't want to find out that an important element is missing or a file is corrupt right as you're ready to go to film. "With the advent of electronic imaging, people think the workflow is much easier than it used to be," says one industry insider. "But to be honest, it's a little more difficult. There's more thought that has to go into it—because you don't have a lot of things in front of you." In the old days (the 1980s!), a prepress department would be working with artboards and mechanicals from the designer. Now typically all you have is a computer file (that has arrived on disk or by modem) and a laser printout. The flaws that might keep a job from printing successfully are not right there under your nose.

But they are right there in the file. So savvy printers make preflighting the first step on the journey.

The preflight technician's main concern is to discover and identify problems. (Strictly speaking, the preflighter does not fix the problems. That would be the job of the file repair technician. But in some shops these roles are more fluid and might all be considered part of the job of a desktop publishing technician.)

Here are some of the things that a preflight technician might spot: Has the customer included all the necessary fonts for the job? Are there missing image files? Does your output of a file match the customer's hard copy? Do the images fit the picture boxes? Do the elements align properly? Is there compatability between the software and the hardware?

Why is this job important?

A customer whose job has printed beautifully and on time is a happy customer. A happy customer is one who is likely to bring more jobs to your company. A company that has lots of work coming in is a happy company. So you could look at this job as a way of spreading the happiness around.

In addition to enhancing customer satisfaction, preflighting also allows the company to recover the cost of corrections. More happiness.

Qualifications

- Comfortability with computers

- Familiarity with the basic terminology of desktop publishing and with applications like QuarkXPress, Adobe PageMaker, Illustrator, and FreeHand

- Strong basic math skills: addition, subtraction, multiplication, division, percentage, fractions, and decimals

- Ability to use a computer network to locate and transfer files and data.

- High school degree or higher (vocational, technical, or art school background recommended)

Rung on the ladder

Entry level

Compensation: $10.00–18.00/hour

Opportunity

It's a good place to start. Most preflight technicians move up as they learn more about the prepress and printing process.

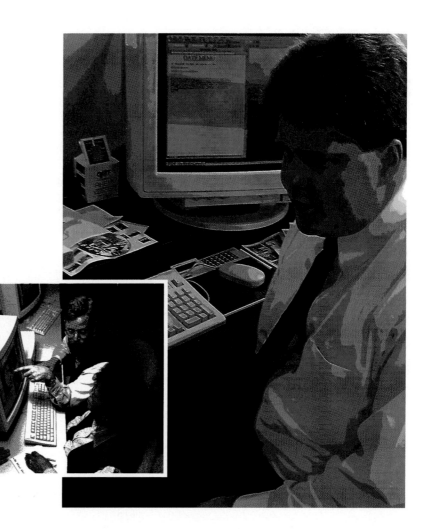

Color Scanner Operator: Making Good Resolutions

In Search Of

Creative, image-conscious individual. Can meet the demands of a fast-paced workflow. Able to come to good decisions quickly.

Check it out

"It's a very demanding job," says a 20-year veteran. "But what I always liked about it was that you got all the glory. If your shift knocked off 120 scans—and they all came out all right—you got the glory." A color scanning operator takes the original image—a transparency or a reflective (the photograph itself, or painting, or other kinds of original artwork)—and follows that image all the way through the scanning process until it becomes a usable digital image. (That digital image is then turned over to an output technician who might place it in a document to be printed, prepare it for publication on the Internet or CD-ROM, or archive it as part of a client's permanent image database. Or all of the above!)

The color scanner operator uses a high-resolution drum scanner, which begins by recording the original (or analog) image through color filters and then using a screen ruling to break the image into dots. Why dots? Well, a photograph or other piece of artwork is what is called a continuous tone. That means that there can be infinite gradations of tones and colors. Printing presses can't print continuous tone. What they can print is an ingenious system of dots. In fact, in color printing, four colors of ink—cyan (a shade of blue), yellow, magenta (a shade of pink), and black—can combine to create most all of the colors found in nature. (This color system, by the way, is referred to as the subtractive process. It is often shorthanded as CMYK.)

In setting up the scan, the operator takes into consideration several factors: what size the image will be reproduced at; what type of printing process it is being prepared for; what type of printing press it will be run on; what kind of paper it will be printed on.

Once the image is scanned, the fun begins.

First of all, the digitized image is evaluated: Does it match the original? Will it meet the customer's expectations? Perhaps the original was of poor quality. Now's the time to fix that. Certain software applications, such as Adobe Photoshop, can be used to perform sophisticated color edits. Color can be manipulated. Whites can become whiter, for instance. Shadows can be made darker. A sexy red sports utility vehicle can become the deep blue that is the latest rage—with just a few clicks of the mouse. "Everybody comes in and they want their pictures to look better than perfect," says one scanner operator. "It's unbelievable what you can do."

Qualifications

- Knowledge of conventional prepress, electronic prepress, and printing operations

- Understanding of color theory as it is used in the printing process

- Ability to distinguish color subtleties

- Comfortability with the major graphics software (Photoshop, QuarkXPress, PageMaker, Illustrator, and FreeHand)

- Understanding of the range of printing processes (lithography, gravure, screen process, flexography)

- High school degree or higher (vocational, technical, or art school background recommended)

- Prior experience in the prepress area

What the pros say

"I like the creative aspect of it. It's not the same every day. Different projects. Different customer preferences. Color is very subjective. What one customer may love, another customer may hate. And it's always fun to take an original and make it look even better."—Brian Schlifke, color manager, American Color

Compensation: $11.00–$18.00/hour

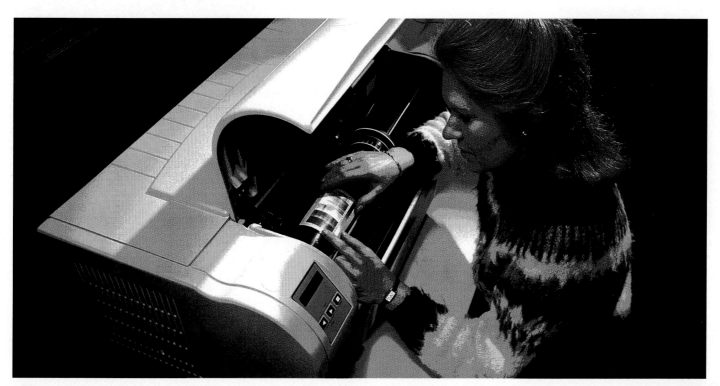

Color Specialist: Showing Your True Colors.

In Search Of
Colorful individual. Must have the eyesight of a hawk—and the personality of a dove.

Check it out
The color show is a critical step in the customer approval process—especially for multi-page printing jobs like catalogs and commercial magazines whose print runs often go into the millions. Color proofs are created—and must be approved by the customer—before printing plates can be made and the actual printing takes place.

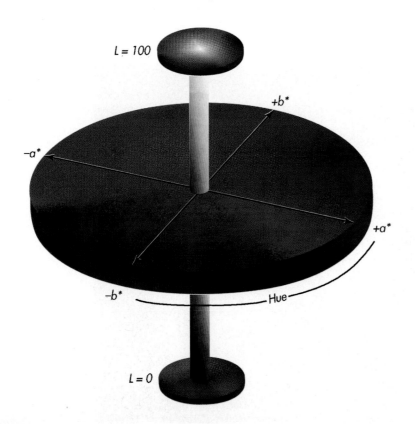

These color proofs—often called by their brand names, for instance, Cromalin, MatchPrint, or Rainbow Proof—serve two purposes. Because they represent what the final printed page should look like, they are judged to see how well they match the original work. Then, once they've met with the customer's satisfaction, they're used as the standard for the printed reproduction when the job is run on press.

"Customers know what they like," says color expert Josette Lankevich of R.R. Donnelley & Sons, one of the nation's largest printers. But, she hastens to add, it's not the customer's job to know how to articulate their preferences in technical terms. That's where the color specialist comes in—as a translator.

"Customers will say things like, 'This doesn't pop,' or 'The blue is not blue enough,'" she says. "These are things that the customer needs to be guided through. What is it exactly that they don't like about the red in a photograph? Is it too dark? Or not dark enough?"

A color specialist uses a small, hand-held magnifying device called a loupe, that allows him or her to see the microscopic dots of cyan, yellow, magenta, and black inks that are combined in the four-color process to create just about any color. "Getting back to this business about a red not being dark enough. You may think just from looking at it with a bare eye that it's too dark because there may be too much cyan in it," Lankevich says. "But if you look at it under the loupe, it may turn out that there's black in there that's making it too dark. And if you take the black down, maybe that's enough. Maybe you can just leave the cyan alone. We're manipulating dots essentially, which is really what process color is all about. It's an illusion. Almost like smoke and mirrors, but it's just dots."

Why is this job important?

Color is an aesthetic consideration to be sure. But there are times when the precision of a color has economic ramifications. "If you're dealing with clothing catalog customers," Lankevich notes, "they stand to lose a lot of money in returns if the color isn't dead on. Or sometimes they'll shoot the item in one color, but it ends up that when they actually get the merchandise in, it's really a different color. So we'll work a lot with their swatches. Or we'll look at the garment itself and see that it is red—but it's not the same kind of red as in the transparency. It's more of a blue red. So we have to add a little cyan and maybe even a little black to darken it a bit."

The color specialist works not only to increase the customer's comfort level but also for the comfort level of the folks back at the prepress center. "When I say 'light minus magenta in a certain tonal range,' they know exactly back in the plant what I mean by that," says Lankevich. "It probably means a 5% move back on the magenta in a certain area. That's not really something that the customer is expected to know. Their job is putting out a catalog and approving the color. They don't need to understand what goes into making the color the way they want it."

Qualifications

- Sophisticated understanding of color theory as it relates to the printing process

- Knowledge of conventional prepress, electronic prepress, and printing operations

- Understanding of the range of printing processes (lithography, gravure, screen process, flexography)

- Prior experience in the prepress area

- Ability to make critical color judgments and fine distinctions among hues

- Understanding of the business and retail worlds

- Ability to communicate clearly with both client and technicians

- College degree recommended

Compensation: $40,000–$60,000

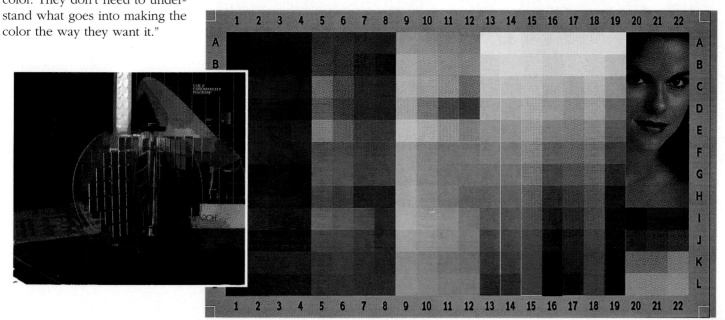

Chapter 8

CAREER CLOSE-UPS
Technical Roles—
Press

Showtime

Presswork is not unlike a fireworks display. All of the conceptualization, design, planning, preproduction work has been done with an eye toward the moment when it all comes together-or, in the case of fireworks, goes off. And presswork does indeed sparkle, speeding along at such dizzying speeds that all the eye can register is a blur of color.

Sophisticated technological advances have been introduced into the pressroom. Unlike the recent technological revolution of the prepress department, however, the underlying principles of printing have not changed. A master press operator or technician, as much as ever, needs to understand the basic operations of a press: dampening, inking, feeding, and mechanical systems, as well the qualities of the paper or other substrates being printed. Today, he or she will also have to understand how to adjust and control many aspects of press operation using a computer console.

Computerization means faster operating speeds on machinery that moved at a fast pace already. Faster operating speeds means making quick decisions. Not much time to mull things over when that press is up and running.

Because experience is something that comes with, well, experience, press operators generally learn each facet of presswork, starting with the lowest position on the press crew. Opportunities to move up through the ranks happen as an aspect of the work is mastered, and as a higher position becomes available.

More than ever, a press operator must have a good understanding of the overall printing process, including the prepress and finishing functions.

Because of increasing computerization of printing press functions, fewer people are generally needed on a press crew. At the same time, the demand for printing is on the rise. The bottom line is that the employment outlook for printing operators is excellent.

and tags the pages and places them on pallets that can hold up to 3,000 pounds of paper where they are ready to be hauled off to shipping or sent on to the finishing department.

Helpers also participate in the preparation of the press during changeover from one job to the next. They might do things like wash out the ink fountains or put the correct inks in the proper units for the next job. They might also change the printing plates and blankets on an offset press or adjust the slitters on a web press that cut the big ribbon of paper.

Most helpers feel that their job is to keep an eye on everything coming out of the press and make sure it all looks good. Often, they're the first to spot a potential problem and communicate it to the press operator.

Qualifications
- Good communications skills

- Mechanical aptitude and measurement skills

- Understanding of the printing process

- Familiarity with flow of work through the presses

- Ability to work as member of team

- High school degree (vocational, technical, or art school background recommended)

Rung on the ladder: Entry level

Opportunity
This is where you start in a pressroom.

Compensation: Minimum wage to $8.00/hour

Helper: All Eyes—and Hands

In Search Of
Alert and energetic person. Enjoys hands-on work. Has a watchful eye and an appreciation for quality.

Check it out
In a pressroom, the helper acts, in many ways, as the right hand of the press operator. The helper's primary responsibility is working the back end of the press where the printed pages come out. As sheets or folded signatures come off the printing press, they must be aligned into stacks. This is called jogging. Jogging can take place automatically as part of the finishing system of the press, or it can be done by hand. Part of what the helper does is make sure this is all happening correctly. Then he or she bundles

Perfecting Operator: In the Middle

In Search Of

Vigilant, level-minded individual. Able to deal with tension; maintain balance. Patience, consistency, and ambition are appreciated qualities.

Check it out

The perfecting operator, also known as the feeder, works with the functional systems of the press, taking care of water, ink, and paper levels. On a standard offset lithography press, for instance, water is a critical part of the printing process. It coats the parts of the printing plate where ink is not wanted. (Remember ink is an oily substance and is repelled by water.) Water is also mixed with another solution such as gum arabic, often called etch, to make the non-image areas of the plate even more receptive to the water and to keep the printing plates clean. One of the duties of the feeder is to watch the level of solution in the etch barrel and to check the conductivity of the water.

The feeder is also in charge of the ink. Different formulations of ink are used for various types and grades of paper and other substrates. The feeder makes sure that the correct ink is set up for each pressrun. He or she also keeps an eye on the ink totes-giant barrels that hold around 3,500 pounds of ink-hooking up new ink totes as the old ones empty.

A third responsibility of a web press feeder has to do with keeping a continuous supply of paper moving through the press at the appropriate speed and tension. A feeder for a web press would also be responsible for splicing a new roll onto the old one as the old one reaches the end. A web press running at a speed approaching 50,000 feet an hour might run through a roll every 30 minutes. So between the ink and the water and the paper systems, a feeder is kept on his or her toes. When there is a free minute, a trusty feeder will also act as another set of eyes and ears, supporting the press operators by checking the registration, quality, and consistency of the pages coming off the press.

Qualifications

- Experience as helper

- Knowledge of press systems

- Understanding of printing process

- Knowledge of flow of work through the presses

- Mechanical aptitude and measurement skills

- Ability to communicate and work as member of a team

- High school degree (vocational, technical, or apprentice school background recommended)

Opportunity

Working as a perfecting operator is the stepping stone to becoming a press operator. In fact, the job title comes from the idea that the person in this role is learning the trade from the press operator, or, to put it another way, is trying to "perfect" themselves for the role of the press operator.

Compensation: Minimum wage to $19.00/hour

Press Operator: Rollin', Rollin', Rollin'

In Search Of

Team captain. Keeps things moving. Able to take in many details at once.

Inspires best efforts in others. Spots problems before they build up.

Check it out

So much work takes place before a job is ready to be printed: A need is identified. A concept is suggested, refined, and finally designed. The project is estimated and scheduled. The prepress department troubleshoots, prepares the electronic files, creates scans and generates film, proofs, and plates. Everything builds up to this moment in the pressroom when the job is finally on press. Everything possible has been done to ensure the best outcome. Now it is all in the hands of a master craftsperson—the press operator.

Makeready is where every print job begins. Plates are mounted. Paper tension is set on web presses. Ink fountains are adjusted. Dampening systems are balanced. For some jobs, especially those run on the more complex web presses, this setting-up process might take as long as four hours. Finally, the press begins to run, slowly at first as the variables are tweaked, and then faster and faster. But even when the presses are running at full speed, the press operator is still making ready—adjusting the inks and dampeners and registration (in color printing, this is the lining up of the image on the plates so that each application of ink is precisely on mark with the others). The press operator is working with a model: the proof that the customer has approved prior to printing. This is the standard that he or she must reproduce.

When the pages coming off the press are to the press operator's satisfaction, the customer is called in to approve. This is called the press check or press okay. Usually there is some back-and-forth since color is subjective. The press operator makes adjustments to the ink fountain keys at a large console and presents printed sheets to the customer, which are then scrutinized and discussed. This process continues until the customer is satisfied with the printing. The makeready stage of the printing process is completed, and the sheets or signatures from this point forward are saved.

The press operator's job is not over, however. Adjustments often take place to keep the printing up to the standard the customer has okayed. While many printing jobs last only a few hours, some are so large that they run for several days. However long the run, a consistent quality has to be maintained. The press operator has to be continually vigilant and spot trouble before a problem develops, with the overall goal of keeping the presses running.

A high level of craft and technical proficiency are critical in a press operator. But there's still more to the job. A skillful press operator must achieve the delicate balance of leading and encouraging the best work from the other members of the team. A master press operator is like the captain of a team. In the end he or she makes the final decisions, and directs the efforts to solve problems, while realizing that a quality product is achieved when the critical thinking and sharp observations of the entire team are valued and respected.

Qualifications

- Previous experience as helper, feeder, and assistant press operator

- Knowledge of features and systems of the press

- Thorough understanding of printing process

- Good color perception

- Knowledge of how press, prepress, and finishing processes interact

- Mechanical aptitude and measurement skills

- Good oral and written communications skills

- Ability to lead a team

- Computer literacy

- High school degree (vocational, technical, or apprentice school background recommended)

Compensation: Minimum wage to $21.00/hour

CAREER CLOSE-UPS
Technical Roles—
Bindery

It's a Wrap

The bindery of a printing plant is a beehive of activity. The work in a bindery ranges from basic manual labor to the operation of technologically sophisticated machinery. Many bindery workers start as material handlers and work their way up. Also, most bindery technicians learn how to operate several different machines.

Machine helpers feed the stitching, folding, and cutting equipment and box the finished product. Handworkers, often employed as needed, do the work of hand-collating and inserting. Stitcher operators may work with the saddle stitcher, which puts wire stitches that look like staples through the center-folds, or the side stitcher, which inserts wire stitches along the side. Folder operators and cutter operators are often dealing with products such as books, magazines, and pamphlets that are printed in signatures—a single sheet that contains 8, 16, or 32 pages—that must be folded in the correct order and trimmed.

Finishing work includes embossing, which creates raised images on paper or other flat substrates; diecutting, in which a custom-made die is used to cut the paper into sometimes unusual and even intricate shapes; and foil stamping.

Other operations that may go on in a bindery include scoring, perforating, gluing, mechanical binding, shrink wrapping, laminating, and drilling. Also taking place in more and more binderies is the selective binding process, where printed products are customized for certain population groups or geographic regions. Ink jet printing has become more popular. It is possible to print anywhere from a few lines to a whole page of text that is customized for specific individuals.

Expect the bindery and finishing operation to become even more high-speed and computerized. Job outlook is good. The U.S. Bureau of Labor Statistics predicts 10,000 job openings each year through the year 2005.

Bindery Operators: The Cutting Edge

In Search Of
Individual who can pull it all together. Appreciates a fine finish.

Check it out
Last but not least. The bindery might be the last stop before a job goes out the door, but it is every bit as crucial to the final product as the two earlier production phases of pre-press and press.

Skilled bindery operators are highly valued. "They can tell you the best way to lay out a job, let's say for a booklet, that can save you money in terms of how much gathering would be involved, or how much folding," says one printing executive. "And if you don't pay attention to them, you might end up costing yourself money."

"They have to be good with arithmetic, too," he adds. "Let's say I have a 24-page book, 7 inches by 9 inches. And I need 7,500 of them. The bindery technician is going

to figure out how he's going to do the fold. He's going to divide down by the size of the form, see how many gathers he has there—and translate that into time. And that's how I price it—based on his time."

As with the other production departments, the bindery too is becoming more technologically sophisticated. Microprocessor-controlled equipment is making its way into more and more finishing departments. Most bindery technicians, over the course of time, learn to operate four or five different machines, developing a broader set of skills and offering more flexibility to the bindery department.

"It's a lot of hard work and long hours," says a veteran bindery operator. "But I would say it's a very good field to get into. There is always work. You'll never want for a job."

Qualifications

- Strong basic math skills: addition, subtraction, multiplication, division, percentages, ratios, fractions, and decimals

- Mechanical aptitude

- Familiarity with the other phases of printing production and how they interact with bindery and finishing processes

- Ability to work well under pressure

- Patience and attention to detail

- High school degree (vocational or technical background recommended)

Opportunity

There are entry-level positions within the bindery, as well as opportunities to assume more responsibility as new skills are learned and mastered.

Compensation: Minimum wage to $18/hour

Bindery Supervisor: End Game

In Search Of

Individual who can make the cut. Quick, adaptable, organized visionary.

Check it out

Put yourself in Bill Schleier's shoes. Bindery supervisor for Williamson Printing Company in Dallas, he might have as many as 20 jobs coming through the bindery at once, or as few as five. Because Williamson is a general commercial printer, the size and nature of each job varies considerably. "It could be 500 saddle-stitch books," he says. "Or it could be 25 million." Either way, Schleier's job is to keep all of the machines humming, keep all of the jobs moving through the finishing department, keep all of the workers busy. It's quite a juggling act.

"You have to keep the cutters working to feed the folders to feed the stitchers," he says. "But there are also jobs that have to be cut and then go right into the box to be shipped out. There are other jobs that cut and fold, and then ship. So you have to balance those with the jobs where the folders are feeding the stitchers to keep the stitchers running. And on and on and on."

As bindery supervisor, Schleier is responsible for all the scheduling for the finishing department. Although he knows what jobs are in the works, he says he can't schedule too far ahead of time. "Obviously you have to look upstream and see what's coming and when you might expect it." But, he points out, press schedules often change, adjusting for

problems that come up as the job moves through the production process. "It's really difficult to try to schedule anything more than 48 hours out because there are just too many things that can happen."

Although most of the work of the bindery supervisor is focused on the last stage of production, he or she is often consulted when the job is in prepress about the most efficient page imposition layout, both in terms of equipment as well as waste. One printing veteran remembers an especially talented bindery supervisor: "He could flow a job through the shop brilliantly. He could take a look at a job jacket and see the whole job—all the steps that it needed to go through. I learned a lot from him."

Says Schleier, "You've got to know the process to be able to help people and determine how best to produce the job depending on the equipment you have and the people you have to run it. In any given job, there's an infinite number of ways to produce it. You have to figure out how best to do it and keep it within the estimate."

Qualifications

- Prior experience in bindery (vocational or technical background useful)

- Thorough knowledge of entire printing process

- Understanding of interconnections between bindery and other phases of production

- Strong mathematical skills and mechanical aptitude

- Ability to communicate clearly with both clients and technicians

- Leadership skills

- Ability to make well-considered and timely decisions

- Management skills

- College degree

Compensation: $30,000–$65,000

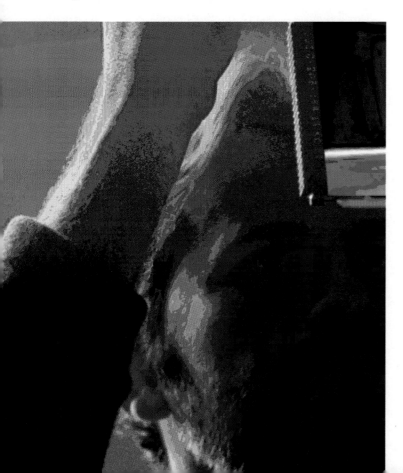

CAREER CLOSE-UPS
Professional Roles
Taking Care of Business

The administrative or professional side of a graphic communications business has positions similar to what you would find in many other manufacturing concerns. There is a sales force that establishes relationships with potential clients and develops business on a local, regional, or national level, depending on the size and the nature of the company.

An estimator is one of the links between the salesperson and production. Estimators calculate the costs involved in producing a particular project, often with several variations so the customer can make an informed decision. Once the company has been awarded the contract to print a job, the scheduler gets involved, establishing an efficient and economical time frame for the project.

Customer service representatives are one of the other links between a salesperson and production. The CSR stays in close communication with the client, working out trouble spots with a project that may occur both on the client side as well as in the prepress, press, or finishing areas.

A graphic communications firm may also employ an accounting staff as well as management personnel, including a sales manager, a customer service manager, a purchasing manager, and a plant superintendent. Another role to consider is that of owner.

Sales Representative: Taking It Personally

In Search Of

Mature, self-starter able to make things happen. Must be personable, able to draw out other people. Travels well. Good listening and communication skills a must.

Check it out

Sales is sales is sales, some say—whether you're selling lumber or vacation packages. But sales reps in the graphic communications industry say the nature of their industry is a little different. "We're selling custom products," points out Jeff Waterhouse of Buffalo, New York-based American Color. "The sales representative, who deals with the client on a daily basis, can be so important. A lot of times I'll have to make a decision on the fly that's in the client's best interest. I need to know their feelings, their taste, their judgments. It's a very personal thing—getting to know them, getting to know what they like and don't like. How they would react to different situations. Knowing what's really important to the client. What's an issue and a nonissue."

Sales representatives have to straddle an interesting position. They represent their company to the client. But they also must represent their client to their company. "I'm supposed to know everything there is to know about the customer—what their business strategy is; what their goals are; how they are growing; what's important to them," says Tom Daly of printing giant R.R. Donnelley & Sons. "How is the customer going to react if we were to move this piece of equipment or close this plant? I'm supposed to be able to represent that customer. I'm supposed to be their voice."

Sales in any industry is built on the foundation of pricing, quality, and service. There are those who would add a fourth base: the ability to act as a consultant. "My goal is to have established clientele that I can help grow," says Glen Ketchian of Banta. "I want to be a solution provider." "You might be able to help them look at their business from a new angle," adds Waterhouse. "You might be able to offer them a new technique that will help to give them an advantage in the marketplace."

"Do as much research as you can," he continues. "Find out as much about your client's business as you can. I use the Web quite a bit to get background on accounts."

Competition among printers can be fierce. Building new business is one of the challenges faced by sales representatives. Maintaining existing accounts, especially in this era of mergers and acquisitions, is another challenge. So what do the pros say are the sure-fire selling techniques?

"Boy Scout traits," says Waterhouse. "Be trustworthy and honest. If you say you're going to get something done for a client, follow up on it."

"Listen well," says Daly. "Understand what people really want. Make sure you have all the details. Investigate until you get the information. And then have the basic understanding to use that information, develop it, and create a solution for it."

Sales reps are likely to be on the road 70% of the time. Travel may be local, regional, national, and even international, depending on the scope of the particular company's business.

Why is this job important?

The sales force is the lifeblood of the company. They are the conduit by which business is brought in.

Qualifications

- Attention to detail

- Strong written and verbal communication skills

- Background in marketing and finance

- Previous experience in some facet of graphic communications recommended

- Ability to understand and work smoothly with people

- Creative, "outside-of-the-box" thinking

- Bachelor's degree or higher

Salary Range: $30,000–$100,000 plus

Note: Financial remuneration varies. Some sales reps are paid straight commission. Others might be paid a mix of salary and bonuses. Newcomers and trainees might expect to be placed on straight salary until they are up and running.

Estimator: And I Quote

In Search Of

Cost-conscious, calculating individual. Knows the value of things.

Check it out

"I feel like an octopus sometimes," one long-time estimator says. When things are really cooking, he says, he may find himself taking phone calls, receiving email and faxes all at the same time. All the while, the message light is blinking on his voice mail. The estimator in a graphic communications company is at the center of a swirl of information—information that he both gathers in order to do his job and that he transmits to others to aid them in decision-making processes.

Estimating is essentially a liaison position, one of the links between sales and manufacturing. In support of the salesperson, the estimator provides the information that will help the salesperson bid competitively on a project. Sometimes that process is pretty straightforward. More often, the estimator runs a number of estimates, each one with slightly different variables. How would the price be affected if you changed the paper width by 1/8 inch? How expensive is it to print in two colors as opposed to four? What happens if you print on paper with a different basis weight? In the end, what a client wants to know is the most economical way to produce the highest quality product.

The estimator also works closely with manufacturing—prepress, press, bindery, and shipping and mailing. In order to produce intelligent quotes on jobs, the estimator must understand the capabilities of the equipment as well as the manufacturing realities and market niche of the plant or plants he or she works with.

"You have to enjoy the dynamics of the situation, the exchange of information," an estimator says. "You have to be reasonably patient. Can't get too excited with the small frustrations. It's a very busy job. The time goes well."

Qualifications

- Prior experience in production or administrative aspects of graphic communications

- Good understanding of materials and production processes

- Familiarity and comfort with computers

- Facility with numbers

- Strong communication skills, written and verbal

- Ability to work well under pressure

- College degree recommended

Compensation: $25,000–$45,000

Scheduler: The Plan of Attack

In Search Of

Are you a big picture person—able to imagine what's just over the horizon? Enjoys puzzles?

Check it out

Imagine the scheduler as a sort of travel agent. The scheduler puts together an itinerary for each printing job. The first thing he or she has to consider is the final drop date—the time the printed piece needs to be delivered to the client or, perhaps, land in people's mailboxes. Working backwards from that drop date, the scheduler calculates when the client will have to have all of their materials prepared and sent to the plant. In between those two dates, lots of work will have to happen. A scheduler's basic charge is to plan the job through all of its stages—prepress, press, bindery, and mailroom. It's sort of like a cross-country trip with lots of takeoffs and departures along the way.

That doesn't sound too complicated if you're talking about ushering one printing job through the process. But remember that printing presses and bindery equipment are sophisticated, capital-intensive pieces of machinery. The way they pay for themselves is by almost constant use. Many printing plants run twenty-four hours a day, seven days a week. The scheduler's job is to find the straightest route (this is what will please the customer) as well as the most cost-effective one (this is what will please the company). In some ways, it's as if you have a certain number of planes—each good for a certain kind and length of journey. And you can only put one passenger at a time on each plane. It takes a lot of planning to keep the planes in the air, get passengers on the best carrier for their journey, and, most important of all, get them there on time.

A scheduler needs to have a good understanding of the printing process and of the different pieces of machinery that are involved. To keep those presses cranking, you have to know how long it takes to prepare a press for a certain kind of job and how long the job will take to run. You have to know what the characteristics are of the different stitchers in the bindery, for instance. It also helps to be observant of patterns—to notice what kinds of things tend to go wrong under what sorts of circumstances.

Not only does a scheduler have to map out a big and complicated itinerary, but the overall plan changes constantly. One press breaks down, say, and the job has to be put on another. Which means that the job slated for that press has to be delayed. Or perhaps the customer runs into a problem and can't get their materials to the printer as scheduled. Change—often hourly—is the constant in a scheduler's life.

Qualifications

- Prior experience in other aspects of production or printing administration

- Good understanding of production machinery capabilities and production processes

- Familiarity with computer

- Ability to solve problems and attend to details

- Ability to interact well with colleagues at all levels

- College degree recommended

Compensation: $28,000–$45,000

Customer Service Representative: Betwixt and Between

In Search Of
Individual to act as go-between; good listener and communicator.

Check it out
In a way, the customer service representative is the social worker of the graphic arts industry. At the heart of this job is the ability and desire to relate to people and their needs.

Customer service representatives, or CSRs as they are most often called, are the folks who take over the project once the salesperson has clinched the contract. They pick up the ball and handle the workflow from beginning to end. A lot of communication among the salesperson, production and mailing departments, and the customer has to take place over the life of any one project. The CSR is the hub of this activity. Let's say a disk comes in from a customer, and the prepress department discovers that the pages are set to output at a different size than the job specifications designate. Is it an oversight? Has the customer changed their requirements? The CSR gets on the phone with the client, gets to the bottom of the problem, and works out a solution that is to the satisfaction of the client.

In fact, customer satisfaction, as you might guess, is the primary concern of the CSR. But it's not as simple a task as the preceding statement might imply. There are lots of things that go into keeping a customer happy, developing a relationship with them that can be long term, and having that relationship be profitable for the company as well. Customers, for the most part, are not printing experts. They can often be unaware of the technical requirements and concerns of producing a job. So one of the things a CSR does is communicate technical considerations and concerns so that the client can make good decisions about the printing of the job as problems arise.

A CSR may be the person who knows the details of the job most intimately. When the project comes in, he or she writes up the instructions and reviews them with the production manager to make sure all of the requirements are clear. When the prepress work is done and proofs are ready to be sent out for the customer to approve, the CSR first inspects them and makes sure they pass muster. He or she might spot-check these proofs against the original hard copy or review the color output. Later, after the job has been printed and delivered, an on-the-ball CSR will check back with the client: Was the client happy with the job? Were there any problems? And perhaps the most important question of all: Where there things that could have been done better?

In addition to being able to communicate verbally, the CSR does a lot of follow-up communication by letter. While customer service representatives don't spend their time out in the field the way that sales people do, most will meet face to face with their customers once or twice a year. That traveling may be local or national, depending on the scope of the company's business.

Qualifications

- Ability to relate to people

- Good understanding of production processes

- Strong computer skills

- Good verbal communication skills

- Strong writing skills

- Some experience being part of an organized team

- Listening and facilitating

- High energy; likes working with people

- Experience in the graphic communications industry

- College degree

Compensation: $25,000–$50,000

Owner: The Buck Stops Here

In Search Of

Hard-working, conscientious individual. Likes to be own boss.

Check it out

"Printing is the last great local manufacturing industry in this country," says Mike Kane, a partner in Benshoff Printing, a medium-sized general commercial printer in Johnstown, Pennsylvania. "In most towns in the old days most things were manufactured locally—furnaces, stoves, radiators. Printing is the last remaining one of them, which I think is kind of neat."

Kane also points out that printing is probably the only custom manufacturing work that most people will ever purchase. That brings challenges that are different from those faced by manufacturers of standardized goods. "It's a little more complicated than selling widgets," he says. "You have to be good at explaining what you can and can't do in terms of maintaining quality and cost parameters. You have to educate the customer a little bit more."

Kane, who entered into the graphic communications business in 1989, says that, at the time, he knew the printing process as a layperson. He suggests that a person considering opening or buying a print shop would benefit from earning a business degree. "You need to have the savvy for the many different opportunities or traps that being in business presents," he says. "And the more you understand technically, the better." Still, he continues, "I think most of the skills—learning how to estimate, or learning how to handle a customer who has a problem—those are skills that you can pick up in a year or two in the School of Hard Knocks."

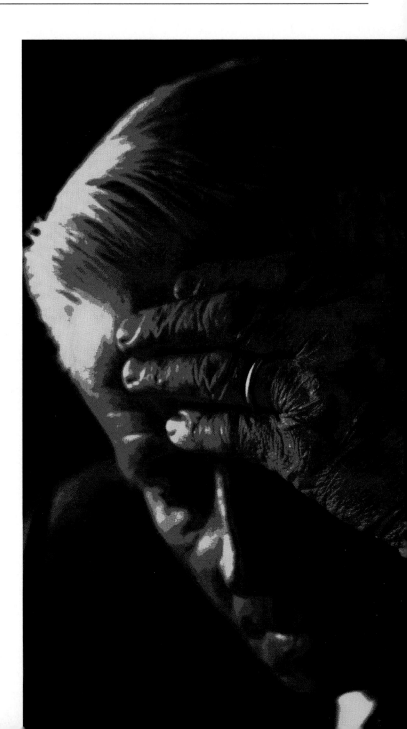

Would you make a good entrepreneur? Kane offers this advice to those considering ownership:

"You need to be able to look inward and outward. You need to be able to look at your own shop and realize what your strengths are. Realistically. And that's a hard thing to do.

"You need to understand how to work in your market—which means you have to have a sense of what your market is. There's a lot more to it than just putting out a sign.

"You need to understand, probably most importantly, what you need your margin to be. And then you need to live with it. Because it will just kill you to give it away.

"You need to understand government regulations. You have to deal with insurance. You have to deal with all the benefits issues and employee relationships.

"You need to understand your banker. You need to have a good relationship with a bank—because you're going to have debt. It's going to be very tough to avoid, just to keep up with technological changes.

"And I think you need to understand that you have to really commit yourself. I don't believe anybody could make a living at this as a hobby. It's too intensive. There are too many things to watch out for."

"You have to have a certain sense of being on a mission," he concludes. "It's not an easy way to make a living. You have to appreciate and enjoy the process of production. When an annual report comes in as a rush job, and you turn it around in three days, and it's right."

"You had all the various aspects of the shop working together, and you coordinated that well, and the people did not just what they were told, but what they knew they had to do because they understand its value to them. When all that happens, and you can tell the employees care and things have been mobilized—there's a great deal of satisfaction in that."

HOW TO GET THERE FROM HERE

One step at a time

Information provides the solid ground that effective career preparation and successful job searches are built on. The good news is that information is plentiful if you know where to look. Start to build a folder. In fact, buy an accordion folder at an office supply store—the kind of folder that has dividers and can expand to hold lots of letters, newspaper clippings, and booklets. Don't consider your career preparation complete until you can't possibly stuff one more piece of paper into this folder.

Look in your phone book and make a list of the printing companies in your area. Put that list in your folder. Next, go to your local or school library and ask the librarian to help you find newspaper articles that may have been written about these companies and the people who run them. When you've found out all you can in this way about the graphic communications industry in your area, it's time to make some personal contact in the form of informational interviews.

Informational interviews are a useful and well-respected way to prepare for a job or career. Call the owner or manager or human resources officer of a few printing firms. Explain that you are considering a career in graphic communications and you'd like a half hour of their time—at their convenience—to learn a little more about the field. Before you go in for the interview, think through what you would like to learn. Do you want to know specifically about one phase of the operation, such as the bindery? Would you like to know how a salesperson spends his or her day? Would it be helpful to understand how computer skills are put to use in the prepress area? Perhaps you would like to see the printing press in action. Most employers will be happy to take the time to meet with you. Not only have you shown intelligent interest in their business, but you've also shown yourself to be a resourceful, self-starting individual— the very qualities they are looking for in a prospective employee.

Speaking of qualities employers are looking for, here are some to keep in mind. Employers say that one of the traits they value most in their employees is flexibility and versatility. "Be willing to learn," they say. The industry has been, and is, changing rapidly. Gone are the days when you learned how to do a job and then settled in for the next 40 years. As the technology becomes increasingly sophisticated, the workflow, tasks, and skill sets change. Employees today are expected to stay current with leading-edge technologies. Life-long learning is the norm.

Whether you prepare for a technical or professional role, much of the work in the modern workplace takes place in teams. The ability to work well with other people is highly valued by employers. What kinds of experiences have you had that have helped you to learn how to work as a member of a team? Have you played sports? Are you involved in organizations through your school or church?

The development of certain skills will make you a desirable candidate for the graphic communications industry. Communication skills—both verbal and written—are highly prized. An understanding of basic math is important, employers report. They are also looking for problem-solving skills and comfortability with computers. Knowledge of page-layout and other graphic software programs is desirable as well.

All in all, the more you can learn about the industry, the better you will understand how to proceed with your career preparation. In this section, we offer further sources of information and resources.

DiscoverPRINT: A CD-ROM Resource

"It's a mixture of art, science, relationship, and technology," explains one young print entrepreneur as he talks about why he likes his chosen field. DiscoverPRINT takes you on a virtual tour through the graphic communications industry. With exciting visuals, it quickly offers the opportunity to explore graphic communication careers in a variety of ways. You can click on skill areas such as math, English, business, sales, technology, and a host of others to see where and how those skills are put to use in graphic communications. If you already know that you're interested in a specific aspect of the industry, you can go there directly to get a sense of particular jobs. Or you might want to take DiscoverPRINT's tour of a printing plant. Information on careers is provided in a straightforward and useful way, much of it through QuickTime video-clip interviews with real people who explain and show what their work is like.

To find out how you can get your own copy of DiscoverPRINT, call the Education Council of the Graphic Arts Industry at 703/648-1768 or send an email to churlbur@npes.org.

71

Internet Resources: Virtually Yours

You're in luck. The Internet and its cousins the World Wide Web and UseNet News provide career searchers these days with a virtual library. Information about the graphic communications industry, businesses, schools, and even jobs is as close as the nearest modem. But the sheer breadth of information can make the process of actually finding it a pretty daunting process. We've tried to narrow it down for you a little here by offering some Internet sources that we think you'll find interesting.

By the way, you might want to learn more about the use of the Internet in the printing and publishing. Here's a good place to start: *Using the Internet and Commercial Online Services: A Guide for Printers* (GATF Order No. 1601). Another good book about Internet-based job searches is *Be Your Own Headhunter Online* by Pam Dixon and Sylvia Tiersten (Random House, 1995).

Printers on the Web: A Sampling

Graphic Comm Central
http://www.teched.vt.edu/gcc

The Graphic Communication Electronic Publishing Project provides a hub for graphic communications educators, students, and industry personnel on the World Wide Web. Its objectives include establishing links to existing information on the Web that will be useful to educators, students, and professionals and converting existing printed educational resources to Web-viewable formats. Publications from the Graphic Arts Education and Research Foundation (GAERF) and the International Graphic Arts Education Association (IGAEA) are available as well as a calendar of Graphic Communication Educational Events. Other resources range from student resumes and portfolios from high school, college, and university graphics programs and electronic mail discussion groups geared toward educators, students, and industry personnel.

Banta
http://www.banta.com

Through its 35 facilities worldwide, Banta Corporation provides clients in 20 market segments with assistance in creating communica-

tions tools for multiple media—everything from book and catalog publishing to CD-ROM development and point-of-purchase marketing programs. A searchable, complete-text version of the second edition of the company's *Technovation Handbook* is accessible on their web site. This book covers new media computer systems, communications networking and data management, and alternative print technologies. You can order a free copy of the print version and review other educational materials, too.

Warren Idea Exchange
http://warren-idea-exchange.com

S.D. Warren, the largest manufacturer of coated free-sheet paper in the world, uses its Web site to foster creativity among graphic designers and art directors. By filling out the Idea Exchange's online form, site visitors can request free printed samples by graphic theme and industrial application from a database of more than 10,000 examples in 120 categories. The actual samples are delivered by postal mail. They cannot be viewed online.

Other site features include surveys, a printers' forum, environmental information about paper recycling, and an "address book" that lists suppliers, associations, schools, and other printing resources. Visitors can order copies of The Warren Standard and other S.D. Warren technical and educational materials, but copies are not posted online. Designers and art directors can also submit samples of their own works to be added to the Idea Exchange database.

Seybold
http://www.seyboldreport.com/homepage.com

Consultants, seminar producers, and publishers of newsletters about the Internet and digital publishing systems, Seybold has created a web site that is a mixture of premium information for subscribers to its publications and other content, including discussion forums, a vendor directory, and special reports accessible to all visitors. You can search a three-year archive of back issues of their newsletters (Sept 93–Aug 96) via HTML table-of-contents links or with the Excite full-text search engine.

SiteSource
http://members.aol.com/nbref/ga_1.htm

Pete Basiliere, a 20-year veteran of the printing and direct mail industries, has compiled SiteSource for Printing and the Graphic Arts, a comprehensive list of over 600 links to printing and graphic communications resources on the Internet. Information is organized by industry segment (printers online, prepress, press, and bindery equipment, etc.) so that visitors can easily jump to areas of interest. Trade publications and associations, consulting firms, executive recruiters, printing museums, and colleges and universities with printing and graphic arts programs are also covered.

Education and Job Information: Sites You'll Want to Check Out

CareerMosaic

http://www.careermosaic.com:80/cm/cm1.html

An international site with job listings as far afield as Korea, CareerMosaic features free resume posting and J.O.B.S. database searching as well as employer profiles and online career fairs. A special "CollegeConnection" section lists job opportunities and entry-level resources for newcomers to the work force. Another helpful area enables visitors to perform a full-text searches of jobs listed in the regional and occupational UseNet (".jobs.offered") newsgroups, which is preferrable to slogging through the thousands of UseNet postings individually.

CareerPath

http://www.careerpath.com

This free site fosters user access to more than 350,000 help-wanted ads from participating newspapers across the U.S. each month. Updated daily, it can be searched by newspaper, job category, and keyword. Employer profiles appear in the form of a searchable database of "mini-home pages" with links to company sites and email addresses.

CollegeNet

http://www.collegenet.com

From CollegeNet visitors can search for scholarships as well as colleges and financial aid information. Other areas on the site feature links to Ivy League and women's colleges and those universities with a reputation for research. Unique among its features is the Web Apply tool by which users who set up accounts can apply to various schools online, even paying for the applications with digital cash or secure credit card transactions. A 3D VRML campus tour is also available, but only of Virginia Tech University.

FastWeb.Com

http://www.fastweb.com

FastWeb.com is a free college scholarship search tool that compares your responses to an online form against a database of 180,000 scholarships and delivers the search results and updates directly to your email box.

JOBTRAK

http://www.jobtrak.com

Of all the job information sites on the World Wide Web, JOBTRAK, which works in partnership with more than 500 college and university career centers across the U.S., is most geared toward the student or recent graduate. In addition to leads on over 2,100 new full- and part-time jobs updated each day, the site includes company profiles and job search tips. It is free to use.

The Monster Board

http://www.monster.com

Use The Monster Board Jobba-The-Hunt personal search agent to access a database of over 50,000 jobs in a variety of fields. The site also offers free online resume building and posting and informative columns by careers journalist Joyce Lain Kennedy.

Online Career Center

http://www.occ.com

Job seekers can post resumes and peruse databases of employment listings by keyword and company information and profiles on this free site, which also hosts open houses, career fairs, and other events. It has an "On Campus" section serving students and recent graduates and another area devoted to cultural diversity. The jobs database covers the United States and more than 100 other countries.

Tripod

http://www.tripod.com

One of the 23 most-trafficked web sites in the entire world, according Mecklermedia's Web Week, Tripod, by its own definition, "is for people trying to live well in a world of constant shift and transition." The weekly e-zine features practical advice about investing and debt management for those saddled with student loans as they join the corporate work force at entry-level wages. Other areas on the site cover health, lifestyles, corporate culture, entertainment, and travel. By responding to surveys and forum questions, site visitors help each other adjust to the pace of life after college. Chatty and humorous anecdotes from Tripod staff members add to the sense of community.

A premium membership with a 10MB home page, a personal chat room, and other gadgetry for the truly Net savvy is available, but, unlike other sites, Tripod's free membership offers valuable content, too. A print version of Tripod, *Tools For Life* magazine, is available as well.

❧NSTF

National Scholarship Trust Fund of the Graphic Arts Industry

http://www.gatf.org

Go straight to the source of financial assistance for students entering the graphic communications field. Scholarship applications can be downloaded from the GATF FTP site accessible through a convenient link. The 300 scholarships are supported by the 41-year-old organization's $4 million endowment. You can also search a list of schools offering certificates and degrees in a variety of graphic communications subjects.

73

Schools:
A Class Act

Education and training, of course, lay the groundwork for a successful career. Schools vary considerably in the way they prepare students as well as the types of careers they are preparing students for. Technical schools and community colleges, for instance, tend to prepare students for technical, production-oriented careers. Many four-year college programs offer students a sound technical base, complemented with coursework in business and management. Graduate programs provide the opportunity to focus intensely on the technical aspects of graphic communications, preparing students for careers as printing technology researchers or educators.

Begin your search for the school that is right for your career needs by writing to them for information. A good second step, after narrowing down your choices, is to set up an appointment to visit several schools. Meeting some of the faculty and other students will help you determine which program is the best match for you.

NSTF
NATIONAL SCHOLARSHIP TRUST FUND

About NSTF

Established in 1956, the National Scholarship Trust Fund (NSTF) of the Graphic Arts has awarded over 5,200 scholarships to undergraduate and graduate students preparing to enter into the field of graphic communications.

Under the control of an elected board of directors, NSTF has been successfully operating for over 40 years. With a total endowment of over $4 million, the investment fees are much lower than would be with smaller investments, and the income earned much higher.

The funds supporting these awards come from corporations, large and small, that are involved in the industry, such as printers, packagers, publishers, press equipment manufacturers, paper and ink suppliers—just to name a few. Donations are also provided by individuals and foundations who wish to support the educational needs of the leaders of tomorrow. By establishing a scholarship, they are able to give something back to an industry that has given them a lifetime of achievement.

When a donor prepares to establish a scholarship, they are given the opportunity to choose how they would like it to be administered. Donors may restrict their scholarship awards to specific schools, regions, study majors, or family members. NSTF will match a qualified student with their stipulations.

Scholarship recipients are selected by a closed panel of industry leaders and educators. The criteria for receiving a scholarship is based upon academic merit and leadership potential. Students' records are reviewed periodically to assure that they are maintaining an acceptable grade point average as well as continuing on in their intended course of study. Students are encouraged to contact their donors not only for purposes of communication, but also when they are seeking interships, coops, and eventually full-time employment.

NSTF offers assistance in industry-wide recruitment efforts in several ways. Two publications supported in part by grants received from the Graphic Arts Education and Research Foundation (GAERF) are available to students and educators. The *Directory of Technical Schools, Colleges and Universities Offering Courses in Graphic Communications* is a booklet that lists institutions offering the courses of study necessary to enter into this diverse industry. *Careers in Graphic Communications: A Counselor's Guide* is a reference piece that explores the different career opportunities available in industry. Both pieces are free of charge and used throughout the nation by students, parents, counselors, and career centers.

Also published each year is *Hire Education*. This book is a compilation of NSTF scholarship recipients' resumes. By publishing their resumes, we are assisting students who are preparing to enter into the work force. More importantly, we are supplying the industry with the names of the best and brightest employees available to them.

To download an application for an NSTF scholarship, visit http://www.gatf.org on the World Wide Web or call 412/741-6860, extension 309 to speak with NSTF administrator Kristin Winkowski.

**Kristin Winkowski
NSTF Administrator**

American Schools
(Alphabetical By Region)

Northeast

Central Connecticut State University
Attn. Sanford Rich
1516 Stanley St.
New Britain, CT 06050
Phone: 860/832-1800

Central Maine Technical College
Attn. Ronald Dyer
Graphic Arts/Printing Technology Div.
1250 Turner St.
Auburn, ME 04210
Phone: 207/784-2385

Fitchburg State College
Attn. Dr. Bucholc
Industrial Technology Dept.
160 Pearl St.
Fitchburg, MA 01420
Phone: 508/345-2151

Franklin Pierce College
Attn. Nancy Stone
College Rd.
P.O. Box 60
Rindge, NH 03461-0060
Phone: 603/899-4206

Gateway Community Technical College
Attn. John Nesklada
88 Bassett Rd.
North Haven, CT 06473
Phone: 203/234-3317, x. 761

New Hampshire Technical College
Attn. Thomas Gonlette
Prescott Hill, Rte. 106
Laconia, NH 03246
Phone: 603/524-5025

New York University
Dept. of Culture and Communications
239 Green St.
Room 737
New York, NY 10003

Rhode Island College
Attn. Dr. Lenore Collins
Department of Industrial Education and Technology
600 Mt. Pleasant Ave.
Providence, RI 02908

Sage Junior College of Albany
Attn. Mick Brady
Fine Arts Division
140 New Scotland Ave.
Albany, NY 12208
Phone: 518/462-8617

Springfield Technical Community College
Attn. Raymond Fontaine
Graphic Arts Technology Department
1 Armory Square
Springfield, MA 01105
Phone: 413/781-7822, x. 3769

State University of NY College at Oswego
Attn. David Faux
Department of Technology
156 Wilbur Hall
SUNY-Oswego
Oswego, NY 13126
Phone: 315/341-2853

University of Southern Maine

Attn. Andrew Anderson
School of Applied Science
37 College Ave.
Gorham, ME 04038
Phone: 207/780-5448

Mid-Atlantic

California University of Pennsylvania

Attn. Dr. Stanley Komacek
Department of Industry and Printing
250 University Ave.
California, PA 15419
Phone: 412/938-4085

Carnegie Mellon University

Attn. Dr. Anthony Stanton
Graduate School of Industrial Managment
Graphic Communications Dept.
GSIA Bldg.
Pittsburgh, PA 15213
Phone: 412/268-2313

Catonsville Community College

Attn. Frank Dingle
Communications Dept.
800 South Rolling Rd.
Catonsville, MD 21228
Phone: 410/455-4984

Drexel University

Attn. Ivy Strickler
College of Design Arts
Philadelphia, PA 19104
Phone: 215/895-2386

Erie Community College South Campus

Attn. John Miliotto
S-4041 Southwestern Blvd.
Orchard Park, NY 14127-2199
Phone: 716/851-1752

Fairmont State College

Attn. Dr. Leonard Colelli
Div. of Technology
1201 Locust Ave.
Fairmont, WV 26554
Phone: 304/367-4156

Fulton–Montgomery Community College

Attn. Joseph Marcuccio
Visual Communications Technology
2805 State Hwy. 67
Johnstown, NY 12095
Phone: 518/762-4651, x. 5011

La Roche College

Attn. Martha Fairchild
9000 Babcock Blvd.
Pittsburgh, PA 15237
Phone: 412/367-9300, x. 177

Millersville University

Attn. Dr. Perry Gummill
Department of Industry and Technology
P.O. Box 1002
Millersville, PA 17551-0302
Phone: 717/872-3316

Mohawk Valley Community College

Attn. Ronald Labuz
1101 Sherman Dr.
Utica, NY 13501
Phone: 315/792-5446

Monroe Community College

Attn. John Owen
Department of Communications
1000 E. Henrietta Rd.
Rochester, NY 14623
Phone: 716/292-3350

Montgomery College

Attn. Fredrick Howell
Printing Technology Department
51 Mannakee St.
Rockville, MD 20850
Phone: 301/251-7530

Pennsylvania College of Technology

Attn. Joe Loehr
School of Integrated Studies
One College Ave.
Williamsport, PA 17701-5799
Phone: 717/326-3761

Rochester Institute of Technology

Attn. C. Harold Gaffin
School of Printing Management and Sciences
96 Lomb Memorial Dr.
Rochester, NY 14623
Phone: 716/475-7313

Rochester Institute of Technology/National

Technical Institute for the Deaf
96 Lomb Memorial Dr.
Rochester, NY 14623
Phone: 716/594-5299

University of Baltimore

Attn. Virginia Carruthers
1420 N. Charles St.
Baltimore, MD 20202
Phone: 410/837-6038

University of the District of Columbia

Attn. Charles Belanger
Printing Technology Department
4200 Connecticut Ave. NW
Washington, DC 20008
Phone: 202/274-5037

West Virginia Institute of Technology

Attn. Jack Nuckols
Department of Printing
Montgomery, WV 25136
Phone: 304/442-3013

Southeast

Appalachian State University

Attn. Dr. Nona Woolbright
Department of Technology
Kerr-Scott Hall
Boone, NC 28608
Phone: 704/262-3110

Central Piedmont Community College

Attn. Jerry Howell
P.O. Box 35009
Charlotte, NC 28235
Phone: 704/342-6794

Chowan College

Attn. E. Dean Gilbert
School of Graphic Communications
P.O. Box 1848
200 Jones Dr.
Murfreesboro, NC 27855
Phone: 919/398-6208

Clemson University

Industrial Education
Graphic Communications Department
Clemson, SC 29634-0711
Phone: 864/656-3447

Danville Community College

Attn. Sheila G. Wright
Printing Department
1008 South Main St.
Danville, VA 24541
Phone: 804/797-8433

Georgia Southern University

Attn. Scott Williams
Department of Industrial Technology
P. O. Box 8046
Statesboro, GA 30460
Phone: 912/681-0190

Lake Sumter Community College

Attn. Glen Ricci
Arts and Sciences
9501 Hwy. 441
Leesburg, FL 34788-8751
Phone: 904/323-3650

Lenoir Community College

Attn. Dwight Downie
P.O. Box 188
Kinston, NC 28502-0188
Phone: 919/527-6223

Mid-Florida Technical Institute

Attn. Tom Lovett
Printing Department
2900 West Oak Ridge Rd.
Orlando, FL 32809
Phone: 407/855-5880, x. 337

Midlands Technical College

Attn. Frances Young
Commercial Graphics Communications
P.O. Box 2408
Columbia, SC 29202
Phone: 803/822-3629

North Carolina State University

Attn. Dr. Robert Pyle
Dept. Of Graphic Communication Systems
And Technological Studies
School of Technology
Greensboro, NC 27411
Phone: 910/334-7550

Okaloosa-Walton Community College

Attn. Robert C. Atwood
100 College Blvd.
Niceville, FL 32578
Phone: 904/729-5313

St. Augustine Technical Center

2980 Collins Ave.
St. Augustine, FL 32259
Phone: 904/823-3637

Santa Fe Community College

3000 NW 83 St., N-311
Gainesville, FL 32606
Phone: 904/395-5804

University of Puerto Rico

Graphic Arts Department
P.O. Box 4800
Carolina, PR 00987-4800
Phone: 809/257-0000, x. 3220

Virginia Tech (Va. Poly. Institute and State University)
Attn. Mark Sanders
Technology Education Department
144 Smyth Hall
Blacksburg, VA 24061-0432
Phone: 540/231-8173

Southcentral

Alabama A & M University
Attn. Joe E. Hudson
P.O. Box 82
Norman, AL 35762
Phone: 205/851-5770

Arkansas State University
Attn. Joel Gambill
P.O. Box 1930
State University, AR 72467
Phone: 501/972-3075

Bowling Green State Vocational Tech School
Attn. Randy Reese
Graphic Arts Department
1845 Loop Dr., Box 6000
Bowling Green, KY 42101

Central Texas College
Attn. Don Donaldson
P.O. Box 1800
Killeen, TX 76540-9990
Phone: 817/526-1349

College of the Mainland
Attn. Sandra Devall
Graphic Arts Department
1200 Kurland
Texas City, TX 77591
Phone: 409/938-1211, x. 254

East Tennessee State University
Attn. Jerry Eggers
Department of Technology
Box 70552
Johnson City, TN 37614
Phone: 423/439-4466

East Texas State University
Instructional Printing
Commerce, TX 75429-3011
Phone: 903/886-5707

Eastern Kentucky University
Attn. Marion Marchant, Ph.D.
307 Whalin Technology Complex
Richmond, KY 40475-3115
Phone: 606/622-1192

Houston Community College
Attn. Roberto Garza
Graphic Arts/Lithography Department
1300 Holman
Houston, TX 77004
Phone: 713/630-7247

Louisiana Technical College—Lafayette Campus
Attn. Wallace Dugas
1101 Bertrand Dr.
Lafayette, LA 70503
Phone: 318/262-5962, x. 227

Mayo Regional Technology Center
Attn. Paul Honeycutt
Graphic Arts Department
513 Third St.
Paintsville, KY 41240
Phone: 606/789-5321

Morehead State University

Attn. Edward Nass
Industrial Education & Technology Department
UPO Box 771
Morehead, KY 40351-1689
Phone: 606/783-2428

Murray State University

Attn. Dr. Thomas Gray
P.O. Box 9
Murray, KY 42071-0009
Phone: 502/762-3394

Northern Oklahoma College

Attn. Randy Long
P.O. Box 310
Tonkawa, OK 74653
Phone: 405/628-6658

Oklahoma State University—Okmulgee

Attn. Gary Borchert
1801 East 4th St.
Okmulgee, OK 74447
Phone: 918/756-6211, x. 295

Southwest Texas State University

Attn. Dr. Warren Mack
Department of Technology
San Marcos, TX 78666
Phone: 512/245-2137

Tarrant County Junior College

Attn. Gerald Shutter
828 Harwood Rd.
Hurst, TX 76054
Phone: 817/444-1394

Texas State Technical Institute—Waco

Attn. Norma Sisemore
Graphic Imaging Systems Technology
3801 Campus Dr.
Waco, TX 76705
Phone: 817/867-3343

University of Houston

4800 Calhoun Rd.
Houston, TX 77204-4083
Phone: 713/743-4089

University of Northern Iowa

Attn. Dr. Ervin A. Dennis
Department of Industrial Technology
1222 West 27th St.
Cedar Falls, IA 50614-0178
Phone: 319/273-2561

Midwest

Ball State University

Attn. Thomas Tomlinson
Department of Industry & Technology
Muncie, IN 47306-0255
Phone: 317/285-5657

Bemidji State University

Industrial Technology & Arts Department
1500 Birchmont Ave., N.E.
Bemidji, MN 56601
Phone: 218/755-2950

Bowling Green State University

Attn. Charles Spontelli
Technology Building
Bowling Green, OH 43403
Phone: 419/372-2437

Central Community College
Attn. Jon Belanger
Printing Technology Dept.
East Highway, Box 1024
Hastings, NE 68901
Phone: 402/461-2478

Central Lakes College—Staples Campus
1830 Airport Rd.
Staples, MN 56479
Phone: 218/894-1051

Central Michigan University
Attn. Dr. Lawrence Fryda
Industrial & Engineering Technology Dept.
100 Ind. Eng. Tech.
Mt. Pleasant, MI 48859
Phone: 517/774-3033

Central Missouri State University
Attn. Joseph Metcalf
Graphics Department
Warrensburg, MO 64093
Phone: 816/543-4454

Century Community and Technical College
Attn. Roger Bailey
3300 Century Ave., North
White Bear Lake, MN 55110
Phone: 612/770-2351

Chicago State University
Attn. Sylvia Gist, Ph. D.
9501 S. King Dr.
Chicago, IL 60628-1598
Phone: 773/995-3764

Cincinnati State Technical and Community College
3520 Central Pky.
Cincinnati, OH 452233
Phone: 513/569-1785

College of DuPage
22nd Street and Lambert Rd.
Glen Ellyn, IL 60137-6599
Phone: 708/942-3029

College of the Ozarks
Attn. Marvin Atting
Graphic Arts Department
P.O. Box 17
Point Lookout, MO 65726
Phone: 417/334-6411

Columbus State Community College
Graphic Communications Department
Attn. Robert L. Queen
550 East Spring St.
Columbus, OH 43215
Phone: 614/227-5013

Cuyahoga Community College
11000 Pleasant Valley Rd.
Parma, OH 44130
Phone: 216/987-5278

Dakota County Technical College
Graphics Communications Dept.
1300 East 145th St.
Rosemount, MN 55068

Des Moines Area Community College
2006 S. Ankeny Blvd.
Bldg. #10
Ankeny, IA 50021
Phone: 515/965-7155

Dunwoody Institute
Attn. Kent Espy
818 Dunwoody Blvd.
Minneapolis, MN 55403
Phone: 612/374-5800, x. 3101

Eastern Illinois University
Attn. Dr. Coddington
School Of Technology
600 Lincoln Ave.
Charleston, IL 61920-3099
Phone: 217/581-2216

Ferris State University
Graphic Arts Department
915 Campus Dr.
Swan 314
Big Rapids, MI 49307
Phone: 616/592-2845

Flint Hills Area Vocational Tech School
Graphic Arts Department
3301 West 18th Ave.
Emporia, KS 66801
Phone: 316/341-2300

Fox Valley Technical College
1825 N. Bluemound Dr.
Appleton, WI 54913
Phone: 608/735-5600

Hawkeye Community College
Attn. Dr. John Sorenson
1501 E. Orange Rd.
Waterloo, IA 50704
Phone: 319/296-2320

Illinois Central College
Attn. Dr. Gary Hinkle
Graphic Arts Department
One College Dr.
East Peoria, IL 61635
Phone: 309/694-5141

Illinois State University
Department of Industrial Technology
Mail Code 5100
Normal, IL 61790-5100
Phone: 309/438-3661

Indiana State University
School of Technology
Terre Haute, IN 47809
Phone: 812/237-3382

Iowa Western Community College
Graphic Arts Department
2700 College Rd.
Council Bluffs, IA 51501

Ivy Tech State College
7999 U.S. Highway 41 South
Terre Haute, IN 47802
Phone: 812/299-1121

Kennedy-King College
Photo-Offset Printing Department
6800 Wentworth
Chicago, IL 60621
Phone: 312/602-5382

Kirkwood Community College
6301 Kirkwood Blvd., SW
Cedar Rapids, IA 52406
Phone: 319/398-4983

Madison Area Technical College
Graphic Arts Department
3550 Anderson St.
Madison, WI 53704
Phone: 608/246-6377

Metropolitan Community College
Graphic Arts Department
Printing and Publishing Technology
P.O. Box 3777
Omaha, NE 68103
Phone: 402/289-1201

Milwaukee Area Technical College
Attn. James MacDonald
700 West State St.
Milwaukee, WI 53233
Phone: 414/297-6433

Milwaukee Graphic Arts Institute
Attn. Lauren Baker
633 S. Hawley Rd.
Milwaukee, WI 53214
Phone: 414/443-6424

Minnesota Riverland Technical College
Graphic Technology Department
1900 8th Ave. NW
Austin, MN 55912
Phone: 507/433-0648

Muskegon Community College
Graphic Reproduction Technology Department
2212 South Quarterline Rd.
Muskegon, MI 49442
Phone: 616/777-0239

Northcentral Technical College
Attn. Jim Marteens
1000 Campus Drive
Wausau, WI 54401
Phone: 715/675-3331

North Dakota State College of Science
Attn. Joen Blouin
800 6th St., North
Wahpeton, ND 58076
Phone: 701/671-2736

Pittsburg State University
Attn. Jesus Rodriguez
1701 S. Broadway
Pittsburg, KS 66762
Phone: 316/235-4420

Purdue University
1419 Knoy Hall, Room 363
West Lafayette, IN 47907-1419
Phone: 317/494-4585

South Central Technical College
Attn. Gale Bigbec
Graphic Communications Department
1920 Lee Blvd.
North Mankato, MN 56003
Phone: 507/389-7293

South Suburban College
Publishing and Printing Technology Department
15800 South State St.
South Holland, IL 60473
Phone: 708/596-2000, x. 2294

Southeast Community College
8800 "O" St.
Lincoln, NE 68520
Phone: 402/437-2676

Southeast Missouri State University
2721 Janet
Cape Girardeau, MO 63701
Phone: 314/335-8632

Terra Community College
Attn. John Foster
2830 Napoleon Rd.
Fremont, OH 43420-9670
Phone: 419/334-8400

Triton College

Technical Arts Department

2000 Fifth Avenue

River Grove, IL 60171

708/456-0300

University of North Dakota

Department of Industrial Technology

P.O. Box 7118

Grand Forks, ND 58201

Phone: 701/777-2249

University of Wisconsin—Platteville

Communications Department

Attn. Virgil Pufahl

1 University Plaza

Platteville, WI 53818

Phone: 608/342-1627

University of Wisconsin—Stout

Attn. Jim Herr

Graphic Communications Management Dept.

Menomonie, WI 54751

Phone: 715/232-1294

Vincennes University

Attn. Ken Whitkanack

Printing Technology Department

PTB-09

1501 N. First St.

Vincennes, IN 47591

Phone: 812/888-4259

Western Illinois University

Attn. Dennis Carson

135 Knoblauch Hall

Industrial Education & Technology Dept.

Macomb, IL 61455

Phone: 309/298-1676

Western Iowa Tech. Community College

Attn. James Van Klompenburg

4647 Stone Ave.

Sioux City, IA 51102-5199

Phone: 712/274-6400

Western Michigan University

Department of Paper and Printing Science

1104 Welborn Hall

Kalamazoo, MI 49008

Phone: 616/387-2804

Western Wisconsin Technical College

304 North Sixth St.

LaCrosse, WI 54601

Phone: 608/785-9150

Northwest

Clover Park Vocational-Technical Institute

4500 Steilacoom Blvd., SW

Lakewood, WA 98499

Phone: 253/589-5573

Highline Community College

P.O. Box 98000

Des Moines, WA 98198-9800

Phone: 206/878-3710, x. 3519

Idaho State University

Attn. Allen Isle

Vo-Tech Graphic Arts Department

Campus Box 8380

Pocatello, ID 83209-8380

Phone: 208/236-3505

Linn-Benton Community College
Attn. Dennis Betchel
Graphic Communications Department
6500 SW Pacific Blvd.
Albany, OR 97321
Phone: 541/917-4998, x. 4545

Lewis-Clark State College
Attn. Penny Osmond
500 8th Ave.
Lewiston, ID 83501
Phone: 208/799-2365

Mount Hood Community College
Graphic Technology Department
26000 S.E. Stark St.
Gresham, OR 97030
Phone: 503/667-7631

Seattle Central Community College
Attn. Kathy Johnson Hougarty
1701 Broadway
Mailstop 2BE176
Seattle, WA 98122
Phone: 206/587-6969

Shoreline Community College
Attn. Brian W. Edwards
Visual Communications Technology Dept.
16101 Greenwood Ave. South
Seattle, WA 98133
Phone: 206/546-4742

Walla Walla College
Industrial Technology Department
204 S. College Ave.
College Place, WA 99324
Phone: 509/527-2712

West/Southwest

Arizona State University
Industrial Technology Department
Technology Division
Tempe, AZ 85287
Phone: 602/965-6685

California Polytechnic State University
Attn. Dr. Harvey Levenson
Graphic Communication Department
San Luis Obispo, CA 93407
Phone: 805/756-1108

California State University—Fresno
2255 East Barstow Ave.
Fresno, CA 93740-0009
Phone: 209/278-2145

California State University—Los Angeles
Department of Technology
5151 State University Dr.
Los Angeles, CA 90032-8154
Phone: 213/343-4510

City College of San Francisco
Attn. Suzanne Korey
50 Phelan Ave.
San Francisco, CA 94112
Phone: 415/239-3481

Dixie College
Attn. Jay Slade
Graphic Arts Department
225 South 700 East
St. George, UT 84770
Phone: 435/652-7855

Don Bosco Technical Institute
Attn. Gordon Young
1151 San Gabriel Blvd.
Rosemead, CA 91770-4299
Phone: 818/307-6560

East Los Angeles Occupational Center
Graphic Arts Department
2100 Marengo St.
Los Angeles, CA 90033
Phone: 213/223-1283

Fresno City College
Attn. Craig Polanowski
1101 E. University Ave.
Fresno, CA 93741
Phone: 209/442-4600, x. 8532

Front Range Community College—Arapahoe Campus
Attn. Ken Black
6600 Arapahoe
Boulder, CO 80303
Phone: 303/447-5212

Fullerton College
Attn. David McCormac
Printing Department
321 East Chapman Ave.
Fullerton, CA 92832-2095
Phone: 714/992-7286

Harbor Occupational Center—LAUSD
Attn. Mary E. Tuck
740 N. Pacific Ave.
San Pedro, CA 90815
Phone: 310/547-5551

Mesa State College
Attn. Suzie Garner
Graphic Communications Department
P.O. Box 2647
Grand Junction, CO 81502
Phone: 970/248-1444

Mission College
Attn. Lin Marelick
Printing Technology Department
3000 Mission College Blvd.
Santa Clara, CA 95054
Phone: 408/567-2803

Modesto Junior College
Attn. Alan Layne
435 College Ave.
Modesto, CA 95350-5800
Phone: 209/575-6335

Moorpark College
Attn. Sexton Stewart
Graphic Communications Department
7075 Campus Rd.
Moorpark, CA 93021
Phone: 805/378-1400, x. 1666

Palomar College
Attn. Neil Bruington
1140 West Mission Rd.
San Marcos, CA 92069
Phone: 619/744-1150, x. 295

Pasadena City College
Attn. Douglas Haines
1570 E. Colorado Blvd.
Pasadena, CA 91106-2003
Phone: 818/585-7250

Pima Community College
Attn. John Mertes
Graphic and Imaging Technology Dept.
1255 N. Stone Ave.
Tuscon, AZ 85709-3030
Phone: 520/206-6322

Riverside Community College
Attn. Terry Keiser
4800 Magnolia Ave.
Riverside, CA 92506-1299
Phone: 909/222-8580

Sacramento City College
Attn: Can Wintner
Printing Technology Department
3835 Freeport Blvd.
Sacramento, CA 95822
Phone: 916/558-2415

Salt Lake Community College
Attn. Steven Manfield
Printing Department
4600 S. Redwood Rd., Box 30808
Salt Lake City, UT 84130
Phone: 801/957-4072

San Francisco State University
Dr. Wan-Lee Cheng
Department of Design and Industry
1600 Holloway Ave.
San Francisco, CA 94132
Phone: 415/338-2211

San Jose State University
Attn. Dr. David Holmes
1 Washington Square
Division of Technology
San Jose, CA 95192-0061
Phone: 408/924-3190

Santa Barbara City College
Attn. John Morrison
721 Cliff Dr.
Santa Barbara, CA 93109
Phone: 805/965-0581

Utah Valley State College
Attn. Douglas D. Anderson
800 West 1200 South
Orem, UT 84058-5999
Phone: 801/222-8262

Warren Occupational Technical Center
Attn. Jane Wright
13300 West Ellsworth Ave.
Golden, CO 80401
Phone: 303/982-8600

West Valley Occupational Center
Attn. Jesus Bastidas
Printing Department
6200 Wininetka Ave.
Woodland Hills, CA 91367-3899
Phone: 818/346-3540

Canadian Schools

Algonquin College
1385 Woodroffe Ave.
Nepean, ON K2G 1V8
Phone: 705/727-4723, x. 5102

Cambrian College of Applied Art & Technology
School Of Communication & Creative Arts
1400 Barrydowne Rd.
Sudbury, ON P3A 3V8
Phone: 705/566-8101, x. 7735

Camoson College
Attn. Rick Caswell
3100 Foul Bay Rd.
Victoria, BC V8P 5J2
Phone: 604/370-3394

Emily Carr Institute Of Art & Design
Attn. Tom Becker
Graphic Design Department
1399 Johnston St.
Vancouver, BC V6H 3R9
Phone: 604/844-3800

George Brown College of Applied Arts & Tech.
P.O. Box 1015
St. "B"
Toronto, ON M5T 2T9
Phone: 416/867-2010

Malaspina University-College
Applied Graphic Arts Department
900 Fifth St.
Nanaimo, BC V9R 5S5
Phone: 604/753-3245, x. 2445

Medicine Hat College
Attn. Brian Thompson
Visual Communications Department
299 College Dr., SE
Medicine Hat, AB T1A 3Y6
Phone: 403/529-3959

New Brunswick Community College—Woodstock
Communications Arts Department
P. O. Box 1175, 100 Broadway
Woodstock, NB E75 5C5
Phone: 506/325-4400

Northern Alberta Institute of Technology
Attn. Larry Bureau
Graphic Communications Department
11762 106th St.
Edmonton, AB T5G 2R1
Phone: 403/963-4850

Red River Community College
Attn. Dennis Pankiw
Graphic Arts Department
2055 Notre Dame Ave.
Winnipeg, MT R3H 0J9
Phone: 204/632-2330

Ryerson Polytechnic University
Attn. Mary Black
350 Victoria St.
Room S52
Toronto, ON M5B 2K3
Phone: 416/979-5050

Simon Fraser University at Harbour Ctr.
Attn. Ann Cowan
515 West Hastings St.
Vancouver, BC V6B 5K3
Phone: 604/291-5074

South Winnipeg Technical Centre

Attn. Leonard Haripiak
130 Henlow Bay
Winnipeg, MT R3Y 1G4
Phone: 204/989-6500

Southern Alberta Institute of Technology

Printing Management Technology
1301 16th Ave., NW
Calgary, AB T2M 0L4
Phone: 403/284-8052

Universite Laval

Graphic Communications Department
Cite Universitair
Montreal, PQ G1M 7P4
Phone: 418/656-7285

Vancouver Community College

Attn. Beth Callahan
250 West Pender St.
Vancouver, BC V6B 1S9
Phone: 604/443-8576

Wascana Institute

Attn. Susan Buck
221 Winnipeg St., North
P.O. Box 556
Regina, SK S4P 3A3
Phone: 306/787-7755

A Selection of Degree-Granting Schools Abroad

Darmstadt Technical College

D-6100 Darmstadt
Germany
Phone: 49 6151 162132

Dublin Institute of Technology

School of Printing and Graphic Communication
Bolton St.
Dublin 1
Ireland
Phone: 353 1 8727177

French Engineering School of Papermaking and Graphic Industries

Domaine Universitaire
461 rue de la Papeterie BP 65
F-38402 Saint Martin D'Heres
France
Phone: 33 76 826900

Graphic College of Denmark

Glentevej 67
DK-2400 Copenhagen NV
Denmark
Phone: 45 31 10 1177

Helsinki University of Technology

Graphic Arts Laboratory
Tekniikantie 3
SF-02150 Espoo 15
Finland
Phone: 358 0 43711

London College of Printing

Elephant and Castle
London SE1 6SB
UK
Phone: 44 171 514 6500

South African Printing College

Printech Ave.
Laser Park
Honeydew
2040
South Africa
Phone: 27 22 794 3810

South Glamorgan (Wales) Institute of Higher Education

School of Printing
Australia Rd.
Cardiff
South Glamorgan
CF4 3DA
UK
Phone: 44 1222 621125

Swedish Royal Institute of Technology

Division of Graphic Arts
Drottning Kristinas vag 47
S-10044 Stockholm
Sweden
Phone: 46 8 790 6042

West Herts College

Hempstead Rd.
Watford
Hertfordshire
WD1 3EZ
UK
Phone: 44 1923 257668

Associations: Network, Network, Network

It's all in who you associate with.

You can use the following list of associations in several ways. First, read through the list and write to the associations that serve special facets of the graphic communications industry that you'd like to know more about. Ask them to send you literature about their organization and particular slice of the industry.

Second, notice the regionally based groups. Contact these. You might ask to attend their next meeting as an observer. Or you might ask if they have a mentoring program. Mentors exist to offer a helping hand to industry newcomers. Finding a mentor in the industry who will take you under his or her wing, describe the industry to you and give you information and advice from an insider's point of view can be invaluable.

Associations Serving Printing, Publishing, and Allied Industries

U.S.-Based Associations

Adhesive & Sealant Council
1627 K St. NW, Ste. 1000
Washington, DC 20006
Phone: 202/452-1500
Fax: 202/452-1501
WWW: http://www.ascouncil.org

Adhesive Manufacturers Association
900 19th St. NW, Ste. 300
Chicago, IL 60611
Phone: 312/644-6610
Fax: 312/321-6869

Advertising Mail Marketing Association
1333 F St. NW, Suite 710
Washington, DC 2004-1108
Phone: 202/347-0055
WWW: http://www.amma.org

American Association of Advertising Agencies
405 Lexington Ave.
New York, NY 10174
Phone: 212/682-2500
Fax: 212/953-5665
WWW: http://www.commercepark.com/aaaa/index.html

American Book Producers Association
160 Fifth Ave.
New York, NY 10010
Phone: 212/645-2368
Fax: 212/989-7542

American Booksellers Association

828 S. Broadway
Tarrytown, NY 10591-5112
Phone: 1-800/637-0037
Email: info@bookweb.org
WWW: http://www.bookweb.org/aba

American Business Press Association

675 Third Ave., Suite 415
New York, NY 10017
Phone: 212/661-6360
Fax: 212/370-0736

American Center for Design

325 W. Huron St., Suite 711
Chicago, IL 60610
Phone: 312/787-2018
Fax: 312/649-9518

American Forest & Paper Association

1111 19th St. NW, Suite 800
Washington, DC 20036
Phone: 202/463-2700
Fax: 202/463-2785
WWW: http://www.afandpa.org

American Institute of the Graphic Arts

164 Fifth Ave.
New York, NY 10010
Phone: 212/807-1990
Fax: 212/807-1799
WWW: http://www.aiga.org

American National Standards Institute

11 West 42nd St., 13th Fl.
New York, NY 10036
Phone: 212/642-4900
Fax: 212/398-0023

American Plastics Council

1275 K St. NW, Ste. 400
Washington, DC 20005
Phone: 202/371-5319
Fax: 202/371-5679

American Printing History Association

P.O. Box 4922
Grand Central Station
New York, NY 10163
Phone: 212/930-0802
Fax: 212/302-4815

American Society for Quality Control

611 E. Wisconsin Ave.
P.O. Box 3005
Milwaukee, WI 53201-3005
Phone: 414/272-8575
Fax: 414/272-1734
WWW: http://www.asqc.org

American Society for Testing & Materials

100 Bar Harbor Dr.
W. Conshohocken, PA 19428
Phone: 610/832-9500
Fax: 610/832-9555
Email: service@local.astm.org

American Society for Training & Developement

1640 King St.
Alexandria, VA 22313-2043
Phone: 703/683-8100
Fax: 703/683-1523

Aseptic Packaging Council

2111 Wilson Blvd., Ste. 700
Arlington, VA 22201
Phone: 703/351-5062
Fax: 703/351-9750

Association for Graphic Arts Training
c/o Lehigh Press—Cadillac
25th & Lexington
Broadview, IL 60153
Phone: 708/681-4695

Association of American Publishers
71 Fifth Avenue
New York, NY 10003-3004
Phone: 212/255-0200
Fax: 212/255-7007
WWW: http://www.publishers.org

Association of Area Business Publications
5820 Wilshire Blvd., Ste. 500
Los Angeles, CA 90036
Phone: 213/937-5514
Fax: 213/937-0959
WWW: http://www.bizpubs.org

Association of College and University Printers
Lehigh University
118 Atlas Dr., Bldg. 5
Bethlehem, PA 18015
Phone: 610/750-3109
Fax: 610/758-5400

Association of Graphic Arts Consultants
100 Daingerfield Road
Alexandria, VA 22314
Phone: 703/841-4811

Association of Industrial Metallizers, Coaters & Laminators
5005 Rockside Rd., Ste. 600
Cleveland, OH 44131
Phone: 216/573-3773
Fax: 216/573-3783

Association of Publication Production Managers
P.O. Box 5106
Grand Central Station
New York, NY 10163-5106
Phone: 212/522-2322

Binders & Finishers Association
408 Eighth Ave., Ste. 10A
New York, NY 10001
Phone: 212/629-3232
Fax: 212/465-2012
WWW: http://www.bindernet.com/bfa.html

Binding Industries of America (PIA Special Interest Group)
70 E. Lake St.
Chicago, IL 60601
Phone: 312/372-7606
Fax: 312/704-5025
WWW: http://www.bindingindustries.org

Book Industry Study Group
160 5th Ave.
New York, NY 10010
Phone: 212/929-1393
Fax: 212/989-7542

Book Manufacturers Institute
65 Williams St.
Wellesley, MA 02181-3800
Phone: 617/239-0103

Business Forms Management Association
316 S.W. Washington, Ste. 7110
Portland, OR 97204
Phone: 503/227-3393
Fax: 503/274-7667
WWW: http://www.bfma.org/~bfma

Chemical Manufacturers Association
1300 Wilson Blvd.
Arlington, VA 22209
Phone: 703/741-5000
Fax: 703/741-6000

Committee for Graphic Arts Technology Standards
NPES, Secretariat
1899 Preston White Drive
Reston, VA 22091
Phone: 703/264-7200
Fax: 703/620-9178
WWW: http://www.npes.org

Composites Institute
355 Lexington Ave.
New York, NY 10017
Phone: 212/351-5410
Fax: 212/370-1731

Continuous Improvement Network (GATF)
200 Deer Run Rd.
Sewickley, PA 15143-2600
Phone: 412/741-6860
Fax: 412/741-2311
WWW: http://www.gatf.org

Converting Equipment Manufacturers Association
66 Morris Ave, Ste. 2A
Springfield, NJ 07081
Phone: 201/379-1100
Fax: 201/379-6507

Corrugated Packaging Council
2850 Golf Rd.
Rolling Meadows, IL 60008
Phone: 847/364-9600
Fax: 847/364-9639

COSMEP, The International Association of Independent Publishers
P.O. Box 420703
San Francisco, CA 94142-0703
Phone: 415/922-9490

Diecutting Information Exchange, Inc.
P.O. Box 115, West Rd.
Manchester, VT 052540115
Phone: 802/362-0062
Fax: 802/362-2861

Digital Distribution of Advertising for Publications
1855 E. Vista Way
Vista, CA 92084
Phone: 619/758-9460
Fax: 619/758-5401

Digital Graphics Association
408 Eighth Ave., Suite. 10-4
New York, NY 10001-1816
Phone: 212/629-3232
Fax: 212/465-2012
WWW: http://www.bindernet.com/dga.html

Digital Printing and Imaging Association
10015 Main St.
Fairfax, VA 22031
Phone: 703/385-1339
Fax: 703/359-1336
WWW: http://www.dpia.org

Direct Marketing Association
1120 Ave. of the Americas
New York, NY 10036
Phone: 212/768-7277
Fax: 212/768-7277
WWW: http://www.the-dma.org

Document Management Industries Association
433 E. Monroe Ave.
Alexandria, VA 22301
Phone: 703/836-6225
Formerly the National Business Forms Association

Education Council of The Graphic Arts Industry
1899 Preston White Dr.
Reston, VA 22091
Phone: 703/648-1768
Fax: 703/620-0994
WWW: http://www.npes.org/industry.html.education

Electronic Prepress Section
Printing Industries of America
100 Daingerfield Rd.
Alexandria, VA 22314
Phone: 703/519-8168

Engraved Stationery Manufacturers Association
P.O. Box 290249
Nashville, TN 37217-1005
Phone: 615/366-1094
Fax: 615/366-4192

Envelope Manufacturers Association
300 N. Washington St., Ste. 500
Alexandria, VA 22314-2530
Phone: 703/739-2200
Fax: 703/739-2209

Federation of Societies for Coatings Technology
492 Norristown Road
Blue Bell, PA 19422-2350
Phone: 610/940-0777
Fax: 610/940-0292

Flexible Packaging Association
1090 Vermont Ave. NW, Ste. 500
Washington, DC 20005-4960
Phone: 202/842-3880
Fax: 202/842-3841

Flexographic Technical Association
900 Marconi Ave.
Ronkonkoma, NY 11779-7212
Phone: 516/737-6020
Fax: 516/737-6813
Email: emcisfta@aol.com
WWW: http://www.fta-ffta.org

Foil Stamping & Embossing Association
P.O. Box 12090
Portland, OR 97212
Phone: 503/331-6221
Fax: 503/331-3928
WWW: http://www.fsea.com

Foodservice & Packaging Institute, Inc.
1901 N. Moore St., Ste. 1111
Arlington, VA 22209
Phone: 703/527-7505
Fax: 703/527-7512
Email: fpiinc@aol.com

Graphic Arts Council of North America
100 Daingerfield Rd.
Alexandria, VA 22314
Phone: 703/841-8100

Graphic Arts Education and Research Foundation
NPES
1899 Preston White Dr.
Reston, VA 22091-1367
Phone: 703/264-7200
Fax: 703/620-0994

Graphic Arts Employers of America
    100 Daingerfield Rd.
    Alexandria, VA 22314
    Phone: 703/519-8150

Graphic Arts Marketing Information Service (PIA Special Interest Group)
    100 Daingerfield Rd.
    Alexandria, VA 22314
    Phone: 703/519-8179
    Fax: 703/548-3227
    WWW: http://www.printing.org

Graphic Arts Professionals
    P.O. Box 3139
    New York, NY 10163-3139
    Phone: 212/685-2995

Graphic Arts Sales Foundation
    113 E. Evans St.
    West Chester, PA 19380
    Phone: 610/431-9780
    Fax: 610/436-5238

Graphic Arts Show Company
    1899 Preston White Dr.
    Reston, VA 22091
    Phone: 703/264-7200
    Fax: 703/620-9187
    WWW: http://www.gasc.org

Graphic Arts Technical Foundation
    200 Deer Run Rd.
    Sewickley, PA 15143-2600
    Phone: 412/741-6860
    Fax: 412/741-2311
    Email: info@gatf.org
    WWW: http://www.gatf.org

Graphic Communications Association (PIA Special Interest Group)
    100 Daingerfield Rd.
    Alexandria, VA 22314
    Phone: 703/519-8160
    Fax: 703/548-3227
    WWW: http://www.gca.org

Gravure Association of America
    1200-A Scottsville Rd.
    Rochester, NY 14624
    Phone: 716/436-2150
    Fax: 716/436-7689
    WWW: http://www.gaa.org

Healthcare Compliance Packaging Council
    1001 G St. NW, Ste. 500 W.
    Washington, DC 20001
    Phone: 202/434-4268
    Fax: 202/434-3446

Hot Stamping Association
    c/o Kensol-Olsenmark
    40 Melville Park Rd.
    Melville, NY 11747
    Phone: 516/694-7773

Institute of Packaging Professionals
    481 Carlisle Dr.
    Herndon, VA 22070
    Phone: 703/318-8970
    Fax: 703/318-0310
    WWW: http://www.packinfo-world.org

Institute of Paper Science & Technology
    500 10th St. NW
    Atlanta, GA 30318
    Phone: 404/894-5700
    Fax: 404/894-4778
    WWW: http://www.ipst.edu

International Association of Business Communicators

1 Hallidie Plaza, Ste. 600
San Francisco, CA 94102
Phone: 415/433-3400
Fax: 415/362-7862
WWW: http://www.iabc.com

International Association of Diecutting and Diemaking

P.O. Box 1587
Crystal Lake, IL 60039
Phone: 815/455-7519
Fax: 815/455-7510
Email: 102741.1173@compuserve.com
WWW: http://www.iadd.org

International Association of Printing House Craftsman

7042 Brooklyn Blvd.
Minneapolis, MN 55429
Phone: 612/560-1620
Fax: 612/560-1350
WWW: http://www.iaphc.org

International Business Forms Industries

2111 Wilson Blvd., Ste. 350
Arlington, VA 22201
Phone: 703/841-9191
Fax: 703/522-5750
WWW: http://www.ibfi.org

International Corrugated Packaging Foundation

113 S. West St.
Alexandria, VA 22314
Phone: 703/836-2422
Fax: 703/836-2795
Email: dicktro123@aol.com

International Digital Imaging Association

84 Park Ave.
Flemington, NJ 08822
Phone: 908/782-4635
Fax: 908/782-4671
WWW: http://pwr.com/idia

International Graphic Arts Education Association

200 Deer Run Road
Sewickley, PA 15143-2600
Phone: 412/741-6860
Fax: 412/741-2311

International Prepress Association

7200 France Ave. S., Ste. 327
Edina, MN 55435
Phone: 612/896-1908
Fax: 612/896-0181
WWW: http://www.ipa.org

International Publishing Management Association

IMPA Bldg.
1205 W. College St.
Liberty, MO 64068-3733
Phone: 816/781-1111
Fax: 816/781-2790
WWW: http://www.ipma.org

International Regional Magazine Association

P.O. Box 125
Annapolis, MD 21404
Phone: 410/451-2982

**International Thermographers Association
(PIA Special Interest Group)**

100 Daingerfield Rd.
Alexandria, VA 22314
Phone: 703/519-8122
Fax: 703/548-3227
WWW: http://www.printing.org

Label Printing Industries of America (PIA Special Interest Group)

100 Daingerfield Rd.
Alexandria, VA 22314
Phone: 703/519-8122
Fax: 703/548-3227
WWW: http://www.printing.org

Magazine Printers Section
Printing Industries of America
100 Daingerfield Rd.
Alexandria, VA 22314-2888
Phone: 703/519-8141
Fax: 703/548-3227
WWW: http://www.printing.org

Magazine Publishers of America
919 Third Ave.
New York, NY 10022
Phone: 212/872-3700
Fax: 212/888-4217
WWW: http://www.magazine.org

Master Printers of America (PIA Special Interest Group)
100 Daingerfield Rd.
Alexandria, VA 22314
Phone: 703/519-8130
Fax: 703/548-3227
WWW: http://www.printing.org

Materials Handling Institute
8720 Red Oak Blvd., Ste. 210
Charlotte, NC 28217
Phone: 704/522-8644
Fax: 704/522-7826
Email: 102512.1772@compuserve.com

National Association of Independent Publishers
P. O. 430
Highland City, FL 33846-0430
Phone: 914/648-4420

National Association of Litho Clubs
6550 Donjoy Dr.
Cincinnati, OH 45242
Phone: 513/793-2532

National Association of Print Buyers
1505 NE 20th Avenue, Suite A
North Miami, FL 33181
Phone: 305/947-5100

National Association of Printers and Lithographers
780 Palisade Ave.
Teaneck, NJ 07666
Phone: 201/342-0700
Fax: 201/692-0286
WWW: http://www.napl.org

National Association of Printing Ink Manufacturers
Heights Plaza
777 Terrace Ave.
Hasbrouck Heights, NJ 07604
Phone: 201/288-9454
Fax: 201/288-9453
WWW: http://www.napim.org

National Association of Quick Printers
401 N. Michigan Ave.
Chicago, IL 60611
Phone: 312/644-6610
Fax: 312/321-6989

National Business Forms Association
See Document Management Industries Association

National Graphic Arts Dealers Association
116 W. Ottawa Street
Lansing, MI 48933-1602
Phone: 517/372-4440

National Metal Decorators Association
c/o Ameripro Management Inc.
9616 Deeteco Rd.
Timonium, MD 21093
Phone: 410/252-5205
Fax: 410/628-8079

National Newspaper Association
1525 Wilson Blvd., Ste. 550
Arlington, VA 22209
Phone: 703/907-7900
Fax: 703/907-7901

National Paper Box Association
801 N. Fairfax St., Suite 211
Alexandria, VA 22314-4326
Phone: 703/684-2212
Fax: 703/683-6920

National Paper Trade Association
111 Great Neck Rd.
Great Neck, NY 11021
Phone: 516/829-3070
Fax: 516/829-3074

National Printing Ink Research Institute
Francis MacDonald Sinclair Memorial Laboratory
Building 7
Lehigh University
Bethlehem, PA 18015
Phone: 610/691-7000

National Scholarship Trust Fund (GATF)
200 Deer Run Rd.
Sewickley, PA 15143-2600
Phone: 412/741-6860
Fax: 412/741-2311
WWW: http://www.gatf.org

National Soy Ink Association
c/o Iowa Soybean Association
4554 NW 114th St.
Urbandale, IA 50322-5410
Phone: 515/251-8640
WWW: http://www.soyink.com

Newsletter Publishers Association
1501 Wilson Blvd., Suite 509
Arlington, VA 22209-2403
Phone: 703/527-2333
WWW: http://www.newsletter.org

Newspaper Association Of America
1921 Gallows Rd., Suite 600
Vienna, VA 22182-3900
Phone: 703/902-1600
Fax: 703/917-0636
WWW: http://www.naa.org

Non-Heatset Web Offset Section
Printing Industries of America
100 Daingerfield Rd.
Alexandria, VA 22314
Phone: 703/519-8156

North American Graphics Arts Suppliers Association
1720 Florida Ave. N.W.
Washington DC 20009
Phone: 202/328-8441
Fax: 202/328-8513
WWW: http://www.nagasa.org

NPES, The Association for Suppliers of Printing and Publishing Technologies
1899 Preston White Dr.
Reston, VA 22091
Phone: 703/264-7200
Fax: 703/620-9178
WWW: http://www.npes.org

Package Design Council International
481 Carlisle Dr.
Herndon, VA 20170
Phone: 703/318-7225
Fax: 703/318-0310
WWW: http://www.packinfo-world.org

Packaging Machinery Manufacturers Institute
4350 N. Fairfax Dr., Ste. 600
Arlington, VA 22203
Phone: 703/243-8555
Fax: 703/243-8556
WWW: http://www.packexpo.com

Paper Bag Institute
505 White Plains Rd., Ste. 206
Tarrytown, NY 10591
Phone: 914/631-0909
Fax: 914/631-0333

Paperboard Packaging Council
888 17th St. NW, Ste. 900
Washington, DC 20006
Phone: 202/289-4100
Fax: 202/289-4243

Paper Industry Management Association
1699 Wall St., Ste. 212
Mount Prospect, IL 60056
Phone: 847/956-0250
Fax: 847/956-0520

Periodical and Book Association of America
475 Park Ave. S, 8th Fl.
New York, NY 10016
Phone: 212/689-4952
Fax: 212/544-8328

Plastic Bag Association
355 Lexington Ave., 17th Fl.
New York, NY 10017-6603
Phone: 212/661-4261
Fax: 212/370-9047
Email: pbainfo@aol.com

Printing Brokerage/Buyers Association
277 Royal Poinciana Way, Ste. 204
Palm Beach, FL 33480
Phone: 561/844-9834
Fax: 561/845-7130

Printing Industries of America
100 Daingerfield Rd.
Alexandria, VA 22314
Phone: 703/519-8100
Fax: 703/548-3227
WWW: http://www.printing.org

Research and Engineering Council of the Graphic Arts Industry
P.O. Box 639
Chadds Ford, PA 19317-0610
Phone: 610/388-7394
Fax: 610/388-2708
Email: RECouncil@aol.com

Retail Advertising and Marketing Association International
333 N. Michigan Ave., Suite 3000
Chicago, IL 60601
Phone: 312/251-7262
WWW: http://www.ramarac.org

Screen Printing & Graphic Imaging Association International
10015 Main St.
Fairfax, VA 22031
Phone: 703/385-1335
Fax: 703/273-0456
Email: sgia@sgia.org
WWW: http://www.sgia.org

Society for Service Professionals in Printing
P.O. Box 25768
Alexandria, VA 25768
Phone: 703/684-0044

Society for Scholarly Publishing
10200 W. 44th Ave., Ste. 304
Wheat Ridge, CO 80033
Phone: 303/422-3914
Fax: 303/442-8894

Society of National Association Publications
1650 Tysons Blvd., Ste. 200
McLean, VA 22102
Phone: 703/506-3285
WWW: http://www.snaponline.org

Society of Publication Designers
60 East 42nd St., Suite 721
New York, NY 10165-0051
Phone: 212/983-8585
Fax: 212/983-6043
Email: spd@aol.com

Society of Vacuum Coaters
440 Live Oak Loop
Albuquerque, NM 87122
Phone: 505/856-7188
Fax: 505/856-6716
Email: svcinfo@svc.org
WWW: http://www.svc.org

Suburban Newspapers of America
401 N. Michigan Ave.
Chicago, IL 60611
Phone: 312/644-6610
Fax: 312/527-6658

Tag and Label Manufacturers Institute
1700 First Ave. South
Iowa City, IA 52240-6041
Phone: 630/357-9222
Fax: 630/357-0192

Technical Association of the Graphic Arts
68 Lomb Memorial Dr.
Rochester, NY 14623
Phone: 716/475-5593
Fax: 716/475-7052
Email: tagaofc@aol.com

Technical Association of the Pulp & Paper Industry
Technology Park/Atlanta
P.O. Box 105113
Atlanta, GA 30348-5113
Phone: 770/446-1400
Fax: 770/446-6947
WWW: http://www.tappi.org

Typographers International Association
84 Park Ave.
Flemington, NJ 08822
Phone: 908/782-4635

Vinyl Institute
65 Madison Ave.
Morristown, NJ 07960
Phone: 201/898-6699
Fax: 201/898-6633

Waterless Printing Association
P.O. Box 59800
Chicago, IL 60645
Phone: 773/743-5677
Fax: 773/743-5756
WWW: http://www.waterless.org

Web Offset Section
Printing Industries of America
100 Daingerfield Rd.
Alexandria, VA 22314
Phone: 703/519-8156

Women in Production
347 5th Ave., Ste. 1406
New York, NY 10016
Phone: 212/481-7793
Fax: 212/481-7969
WWW: http://www.wip.org

XPLOR International
   The Electronic Document Systems Association
   24238 Hawthorn Blvd.
   Torrance, CA 90505-6505
   Phone: 310/373-3633
   Fax: 310/375-4240
   WWW: http://www.xplor.org

U.S. Regional Networking Groups

Advertising Club of Kansas City
   9229 Ward Pky., Ste. 260
   Kansas City, MO 64114-3311
   Phone: 816/822-0300
   Fax: 816/822-1840
   Email: basclub@sprintmail.com

Advertising Club of Metro Washington
   7200 Wisconsin Ave., Ste. 200
   Bethesda, MD 20814
   Phone: 301/656-2582
   Fax: 301/904-3307

**Association of Graphic Communications
(New York/New Jersey) PIA**
   330 Seventh Ave., 9th Fl.
   New York, NY 10001-5010
   Phone: 212/279-2100
   Fax: 212/279-5381
   Center for Graphic Communications Education
   Phone: 212/279-2111

Baltimore Publishers Association
   P.O. Box 5584
   Baltimore, MD 21285
   Phone: 410/313-9338

BookBuilders of Boston
   27 Wellington Dr.
   Westwood, MA 02181-4007
   Phone: 617/461-0298

Bookbuilders of Washington
   P.O. Box 23805
   Washington, DC 20026
   Phone: 202/287-3738

Bookbuilders West
   P.O. Box 7046
   San Francisco, CA 94120-9727
   Phone: 510/642-5394
   WWW: http://www.bookbuilders.org

Chicago Association of Direct Marketing
   200 N. Michigan Ave., Suite 30
   Chicago, IL 60601
   Phone: 312/541-1272

Chicago Book Clinic
   11 LaSalle St., Ste. 1400
   Chicago, IL 60603
   Phone: 312/553-2200

Chicago Women in Publishing
   200 N. Washington, Suite 201
   Chicago, IL 60540
   Phone: 312/641-6311
   Fax: 312/416-3860

Direct Marketing Association of Detroit
   30800 Telegraph Rd., Ste. 1724
   Birmingham, MI 48025
   Phone: 810/258-8803

Florida Magazine Association
   P.O. Box 150127
   Altamonte Spring, FL 23715-0127
   Phone: 407/774-7880

Florida Publishers Association

P.O. Box 430

Highland City, FL 33846-0430

Phone: 941/648-4420

Graphic Arts Association (SE PA and DE)/PIA

1900 Cherry St.

Philadelphia, PA 19103

Phone: 215/299-3300

WWW: http://www.gaa1900.com

Graphic Communications Industries Association of Oklahoma/PIA

5200 South Yale, Suite 201

Tulsa, OK 74135

Phone: 918/481-8784

Fax: 918/481-8752

Mid-America Book Publishers

P.O. Box 30242

Lincoln, NE 68503-0242

Phone: 402/466-9665

Pacific Press Publishing Association

P.O. Box 7000

Boise, ID 83707

Phone: 208/465-2500

WWW: http://www.pacificpress.com

Pacific Printing & Imaging Association (of Washington)/PIA

Canal Place

180 Nickerson, Ste. 102

Seattle, WA 98109

Phone: 206/285-8361

Fax: 206/282-0447

Pacific Printing & Imaging Association (of Oregon)/PIA

5319 SW Westgate Dr., Ste. 117

Portland, OR 97221

Phone: 503/297-3328

Fax: 503/297-3320

Philadelphia Book Clinic

136 Chester Ave.

Yeardon, PA 19050-3831

Phone: 215/259-7022

Print Buyers Association (Northern Calif.)

665 3rd St., Suite 500

San Francisco, CA 94107-1990

Phone: 415/495-8242

WWW: http://www.pinc.com

Printing & Graphic Communications Association (Metro Washington) PIA

1333 "H" St. NW

Seven West Tower

Washington, DC 20005-4707

Phone: 202/682-3001

Fax: 202/842-0980

Printing & Imaging Association of the Mountain States/PIA

5031 S. Ulster St., Ste. 350

Denver, CO 80237-2804

Phone: 303/771-1578

Fax: 303/771-2945

Printing & Imaging Association of New York State/PIA

636 North French Rd., Suite 1

Amherst, NY 14228

Phone: 716/691-3211

Fax: 716/691-4249

Printing & Imaging Association of Texas/PIA

910 W. Mockingbird Ln.

Dallas, TX 75247

Phone: 214/630-8871

Fax: 214/688-1767

Printing Association of Florida/PIA

6250 Hazeltine National Dr., Suite 114

Orlando, FL 32822-8333

Phone: 407/240-8009

Fax: 407/240-8333

WWW: http://www.pwr.com/printpaf

Printing Association of (Northern) Florida
215 S. Monroe St., Ste. 350
Tallahassee, FL 32301-1802
Phone: 904/681-9237
Fax: 904/681-9631

Printing Association of (Southern) Florida
6095 N.W. 167th St., Ste. D7
Miami, FL 33015
Phone: 305/558-4855
Fax: 305/823-8965

Printing Industries Association of Arizona/PIA
4315 N. 12th St., Ste. 200
Phoenix, AZ 85014-4523
Phone: 602/265-7742
Fax: 602/265-8259

Printing Industries Association of the Heartland
250 Richards Rd., Ste. 267
Kansas City, MO 64105
Phone: 816/421-7677
Fax: 816/421-7073

Printing Industries Association (Central Ohio)/PIA
88 Dorchester Sq., P.O. Box 819
Westerville, OH 43086-3350
Phone: 614/794-2300
Fax: 614/794-2049

Printing Industries Association (Northern Ohio)/PIA
30400 Detroit Rd., Ste. 206
Cleveland, OH 44145-1855
Phone: 216/835-6900
Fax: 216/835-4121

Printing Industries Association of San Diego/PIA
3914 Murphy Canyon Rd., Ste. A-226
San Diego, CA 92123-4423
Phone: 619/571/6555
Fax: 619/571-7935

Printing Industries Association of Southern California/PIA
P.O. Box 91-1151
Los Angeles, CA 90091-1151
Phone: 213/728-9500
Fax: 213/724-2327

Printing Industries Association of the South/PIA
P.O Box 290249
Nashville, TN 37229-0249
Phone: 615/366-1094
Fax: 615/366-4192

Printing Industries Association (Southern Ohio)/PIA
11 Triangle Park Dr.
Cincinnati, OH 45246
Phone: 513/771-5422
Fax: 513/771-5425

Printing Industries of Michigan/PIA
23815 Northwestern Hwy., Ste.2700
Southfield, MI 48075-7713
Phone: 810/354-9200
Fax: 810/354-1711

Printing Industries of New England/PIA
10 Tech. Cir., P.O. Box 2009
Natick, MA 01760-0015
Phone: 508/655-8700
Fax: 508/655-2586
WWW: http://www.pine.org

Printing Industries of Northern California/PIA
665 Third St., Ste. 500
San Francisco, CA 94107-1990
Phone: 415/495-8242
Fax: 415/543-7790
WWW: http://www.pic.net.com/

Printing Industries of St. Louis/PIA

Joseph White Building
1790 S. Brentwood Blvd.
St. Louis, MO 63144-1312
Phone: 314/962-6780
Fax: 314/962-4490

Printing Industries of the Gulf Coast/PIA

1324 W. Clay St.
Houston, TX 77019-4004
Phone: 713/522-2064
Fax: 713/522-8342

Printing Industries of the Midlands/PIA

4430 114th St.
Urbandale, IA 50322-5409
Phone: 800/397-0733
Fax: 515/270-8701

Printing Industries of Utah

445 E. Second St., Ste.16
Salt Lake, UT 84111-2162
Phone: 801/521-2623
Fax: 801/532-3820

Printing Industries of Virginia

1108 E. Main St., Ste. 300
Richmond, VA 23219-3530
Phone: 804/643-1800
Fax: 804/642-7482

Printing Industries of Wisconsin

P.O. Box 126
Elm Grove, WI 53122-0126
Phone: 414/785-9090
Fax: 414/785-7043

Printing Industry Association of Connecticut & Western Massachusetts/PIA

One Regency Dr., P.O. Box 30
Bloomfield, CT 06002-0030
Phone: 203/242-8991
Fax: 203/286-0787

Printing Industry Association of Georgia/PIA

5020 Highlands Pkwy.
Smyrna, GA 30082
Phone: 404/433-3050
Fax: 404/433-3062

Printing Industry Association of Western Pennsylvania

212 Ninth St., Ste. 500
Pittsburgh, PA 15222
Phone: 412/281-0400
Fax: 412/281-0470

Printing Industry of Connecticut/PIA

P.O. Box 144
Milford, CT 06460
Phone: 203/874-6793
Fax: 203/874-0291

Printing Industry of Illinois/Indiana Association/PIA

70 E. Lake St.
Chicago, IL 60601
Phone: 312/704-5000
Fax: 312/704-5025

Printing Industry of Maryland/PIA

2045 York Rd., Second Fl.
Timonium, MD 21093-4230
Phone: 800/560-3306
Fax: 410/560-3305

Printing Industry of Minnesota/PIA

2829 University Ave. SE, Ste. 750
Minneapolis, MN 55414-3222
Phone: 612/379-3360
Fax: 612/379-6030

Printing Industry of the Carolinas/PIA

P.O. Box 19889

Charlotte, NC 28219-0889

Phone: 704/357-1150

Fax: 704/357-1154

Print/New Jersey

75 Kearny Ave.

P.O. Box 6

Kearny, NJ 07032

Phone: 201/997-7468

Publication Production Association of Southern California

P.O. Box 15305

Long Beach, CA 90815-0305

Phone: 310/425-1721

Publication Production Club (Midwest)

c/o Hunter Publishing

2101 Arlington Heights Rd., #105

Arlington Heights, IL 60005-4142

Phone: 708/427-9512

Western Publications Association

823 Rim Crest Drive

Westlake Village, CA 91361

Phone: 805/495-1863

Fax: 805/497-1849

Wisconsin Publisher Production Club

P.O. Box 299

Edgertown, WI 53534

Phone: 608/838-9899

WWW: http://www.tradpre.com/wppc

Women's Ad Club of Chicago

30 N. Michigan Ave., Ste. 508

Chicago, IL 60602

312/263-2215

Young Printing Executives of New York

Five Penn Plaza

New York, NY 10001

Phone: 212/279-2110

Canadian Associations

Association Des Arts Graphiques du Quebec/PIA

65 rue de Castelnauo

Bureau 101

Montreal, PQ H2R 2W3

Phone: 514/274-7446

Fax: 514/274-7482

British Columbia Printing Industries Association/PIA

409 Granville St., Suite 523

Vancouver, BC V6C 1T2

Phone: 604/683-5858

Fax: 604/669-5343

Canadian Book Publishers Council

250 Merton St., Ste. 203

Toronto, ONT M4S 1B1

Phone: 416/322-7011

Fax: 416/322-6999

Canadian Business Forms Association

75 Albert St., Ste. 906

Ottawa, ONT K1P 5E7

Phone: 613/236-7208

Fax: 613/236-8169

Canadian Plastics Institute
5925 Airport Rd., Ste. 515
Mississauga, ONT L4V 1W1
Phone: 905/612-9997

Canadian Printing Industries Association/PIA
75 Albert St.
Fuller Bldg., Ste. 906
Ottawa , ONT K1P 5E7
Phone: 613/236-7208
Fax: 613/236-8169

Canadian Pulp & Paper Association
1155 Metcalfe St.
2300 Sun-Life Building
Montreal, PQ H3B 2X9
Phone: 514/866-6621

Nova Scotia Printing Industries Association/PIA
P.O. Box 82
Enfield, NS B2T 1C6
Phone: 902/883-1500
Fax: 902/883-8586

Ontario Printing & Imaging Association/PIA
6420 Kestrel Rd.
Mississauga, ON L5T 1Z7
Phone: 905/564-9411
Fax: 905/564-9413

Printing & Graphics Industries Association of Alberta/PIA
Box 21006, Dominion Postal Outlet
Calgary, AB T2P 4H5
Phone: 403/281-1421
Fax: 403/251-6702

Saskatchewan Graphic Arts Industries Association/PIA
P.O. Box 7152
Saskatoon, SK S7K 4J1
Phone: 306/242-9146
Fax: 306/242-9174

Mexican, Central and South American Associations

Association of Graphic Arts Industries
Edificio Camara de Industriales
Esquinia Puenta Anauco
Pte. Republica
Caracas
Venezuela

Association of Graphic Industries of Ecuador
Calle Acuna No 167
Quito
Ecuador

Association of Graphic Industries of Paraguay
Calle Ayolas 162/31
Asuncion
Paraguay

Association of National Graphics Industries of Colombia
Carrera 4A No 25B - 12
Bogota
Colombia

Association of Printing in Uruguay
Ciudadela 1410
Montevideo
Uruguay

Bolivian Graphics Industries Association
Edificio "El Condor" 4to Piso, Oficina 408
La Paz
Bolivia

Brazilian Graphics Association
    Rua Marques de Itu, 7o - 120 andar
    Sao Paulo
    Brazil

Chilean Printing Association
    Canada 253 Depto. C
    Santiago
    Chile

Chilean Publishers Association
    Alameda Lib Bdo O'Higgins 1370
    Of 501
    Santiago 13.526
    Chile
    Phone: 56 2 672 4088
    Fax: 56 41 237 679

Chilean Pulp and Paper Technical Association
    Lincoyan 199 2o Piso
    Concepcion
    Casilla 74c
    Chile
    Phone: 56 41 241 248
    Fax: 56 41 237 679

Confederation of Latin American Graphics Industries
    CONLATINGRAF
    Technical Department
    Canada 253 Dpto. C
    Casilla 166/3 Santiago
    Chile

Federation of Argentinian Graphics Industries
    Calle Ramon L. Falcon No 1657
    Buenos Aires
    Argentina

Mexican National Association of the Graphic Arts Industries
    Canagraf
    Av. Rio Churubusco No. 428
    Col. Del Carmen Coyoacan 04100
    Mexico D.F.
    Phone: 659 15 20
    Fax: 554 3535

Peruvian Association of Graphics and Printing
    Av. Inca Garcilaso de la Vega 1494
    2do Piso Lima
    Peru

Asian/Pacific Rim Associations

All India Federation of Master Printers
    E-14, 3rd Floor
    NDSE Market Part - II
    New Delhi 110 049
    India
    Phone: 91 11 644 2646
    Fax: 91 11 644 9855

All Japan Printing Industry Association
    Nippon Insatusu Kaikan
    1-16-3 Shintomi
    Chuo-Ku, 104
    Japan
    Phone: 81 3 352 24571
    Fax: 81 3 355 27727

All Japan Printing Type Industry Association
    2-11-13 Misakicho
    Chiyoda-ku
    Tokyo 101
    Japan
    Phone: 81 3 265 3786

Australian Book Publishers Association
89 Jones St.
Suite 59/60
Level 3
Ultimo NSW 2007
Australia
Phone: 61 2 281 9788
Fax: 61 2 281 1073

Australian Business Forms Association
77 Lithgow Street
St. Leonards NSW 2065
Australia
Phone: 61 2 438 2777
Fax: 61 2 439 2405

Bombay Master Printers Association
216 Neelam
108 Worli Seaface Road
Bombay 400 018
India
Phone: 91 22 493 4654

China Technical Association of the Paper Industry
12 Guanghua Road
Beijing 100020
Peoples' Republic of China
Phone: 86 1 500 2880
Fax: 86 1 500 4461

Designers Institute of New Zealand
P.O. Box 5521
Wellesley Street
Auckland
New Zealand
Phone: 64 09 771 273
Fax: 64 09 771 272

Graphic Arts Services Association of Australia
356 Liverpool Road
Ashfield Sydney NSW 2131
Australia
Phone: 61 2 716 7633
Fax: 61 2 716 6253

Hong Kong Graphic Arts Association
TST
P.O. Box 91073
Kowloon
Hong Kong

Hong Kong Printers Association
First Floor
48-50 Johnston Road
Wanchain
Hong Kong
Phone: 852 5 271859
Fax: 8610463

Japan Association of Graphic Arts Technology
1-29-11 Wada
Suginami-ku
Tokyo 166
Japan
Phone: 81 3 384 3111

Japan Graphic Designers Association
Jagda Building
2-27-14 Jingumae Shibuya-ku
Tokyo 150
Japan
Phone: 81 3 3404 2557
Fax: 81 3 3404 2554

Japan Light Printing Industry Association
3-2 Jimbocho Kanda
Chiyoda-ku
Tokyo 101
Japan
Phone: 81 3 263 5235

Japan Printing, Bookbinding, and Paper Converting Machinery Industry Association

Kikai Shinko Kaikan Building 3-5-8
Shiba-koen
Minato-ku
Tokyo 105
Japan
Phone: 81 3 434 44661
Fax: 81 3 434 0301

Japan Printing Ink and Varnishmakers Association

2-1-1 Minamikyutaromachi
Higashiku
Osaka 541
Japan
Phone: 81 6 262 5548

Japan Printing Inkmakers Association

Tokyo Club Building 5F
3-2-6 Kasumigaseki
Chiyoda-ku
Tokyo 100
Japan
Phone: 81 3 580 0876

Japanese Society of Printing Science and Technology

1-16-8 Shintomi
Chuo-ku
Tokyo
Japan

Japan Technical Association of the Pulp and Paper Industry

Kami Pulp Kaikan Building
9-11 Ginza 3-chrome
Chuo-ku
Tokyo 104
Japan
Phone: 81 3 541 8204
Fax: 81 3 541 8354

Lithographic Institute of Australia

Federal Headquarters
P.O. Box Q36
Queen Victoria Bldg.
Sydney NSW 2001
Australia

Printing and Allied Trades Employers' Federation of Australia

77 Lithgow St.
P.O. Box 58
St. Leonards NSW 2065
Australia
Phone: 61 2 372 1222
Fax: 61 2 439 2405

Printing Industries Association of Australia

77 Lithgow St.
St. Leonards NSW 2065
Phone: 02 972 1222
Fax: 02 972 1288

Printing Industries Federation of New Zealand

P.O. Box 1422, G.P.O.
Wellington
New Zealand
Phone: 64 4 723 497
Fax: 64 4 723 534

Printing Industries Federation of South Africa

P.O. Box 1084
Honeydew 2040
South Africa
Phone: 27 11 794 3810
Fax: 27 11 794 3964

Pulp and Paper Manufacturers Federation of Australia
P.O. Box 1469N
Melbourne VIC 3001
Australia
Phone: 61 3 698 4207
Fax: 61 3 690 1180

Screen Printers Association of Australia
P.O. Box 10
Northgate Queensland 4013
Australia
Phone: 61 7 266 7033

Screen Printing Association International of Japan
36-11 Hakusan 4-chrome
Bunkyo-ku
Tokyo 112
Japan

Screen Printing Merchants Association of Hong Kong
Block A
New Port Industrial and Commercial Centre 3/F
Kowloon
Hong Kong
Phone: 852 3 654770

Singapore Master Printers Association
68 Lorong 16 Geylang
#04-02 Association Building
1439
Singapore
Phone: 65 745 6913
Fax: 65 745 6916

South African Screen Printing Association
P.O. Box 1200
Johannesburg 2000
South Africa
Phone: 27 11 838 6656

Technical Association of the Australian and New Zealand Pulp and Paper Industries
255 Drummond St., Suite 47, Level 1
Carlton Clocktower
Carlton VIC 3053
Australia
Phone: 61 3 347 2377
Fax: 61 3 348 1206

Thai Lac (Ink) Association
66 Chalerm Khetr
Bangkok 1
Thailand

European Associations

Association for the Promotion of Research in the Graphic Arts Industry
See UGRA

Association for the Study and Application
of Graphics Technology
Barquillo no 11 - 4 D
E-28004 Madrid
Spain
Phone: 34 522 9084
Fax: 34 522 7249

Association of Dutch Designers
Het Arsenaal
Waterlooplein 219
NL-1011 PG Amsterdam
Netherlands
Phone: 31 20 624 4748
Fax: 31 20 627 8585

Association of German Bookbinders Guilds

Heinrichsalle 72
W-5100 Aachen
Germany
Phone: 49 241 532709
Fax: 49 241 509080

Association of German Bookbinding Companies

Jessenstrasse 4
W-2000 Hamburg 50
Germany
Phone: 49 40 381717

Association of Master Printers of Luxembourg

2 Circuit de la Foire Internationale
BP 1604
L-1016
Luxembourg
Phone: 352 42 45 1122

Association of Italian Screen Printers

via Papcino 4
1-10121 Torino
Italy
Phone: 39 11 276 495

Austrian Association of Graphic Designers, Illustrators, and Product Designers

Schonbrunner Strasse 38/8
A-1050 Vienna
Austria
Phone: 43 1 587 6501
Fax: 43 1 586 0575

Austrian Association of Graphic Enterprises

Gruangergasse 4
A-1010 Vienna
Austria
Phone: 43 1 512 6609
Fax: 43 1 513 2826-19

Austrian Association of Newspaper Publishers and Printers

Schreyvogelgasse 3
A-1010 Vienna
Austria
Phone: 43 1 533 6178
Fax: 43 1 533 6178-22

Austrian Booksellers and Publishers Association

Grunangergasse4
A-1010 Vienna
Austria
Phone: 43 1 512 6609
Fax: 43 1 513 2826-19

Austrian Prepress Association

Grunangergasse 4
A-1010 Vienna
Austria
Phone: 43 1 512 6609
Fax: 43 1 513 2826-19

Austrian Research Organization of the Graphic Arts Industry

Leyerstrasse 6
A-1140 Vienna
Austria
Phone: 43 1 922 6542-1
Fax: 43 1 9641-10

Belgian Coatings Research Institute

Avenue Pierre Holoffe
B-1342 Limelette
Belgium
Phone: 32 2 653 0986
Fax: 32 2 653 9503

Belgian Publishers Association
Boulevard Lambermont 140
Boite 1
B-1030 Brussels
Belgium
Phone: 32 2 241 6580
Fax: 32 2 216 7131

Belgian Screen Printers Association
F Neuraystraat 40
B-1060 Brussels
Belgium
Phone: 32 2 134 30748

British Association of Print and Copyshops
3-5 North Street
Great Dunmow
Essex   CM61AZ
UK
Phone: 44 1371 874911

British Printing Industries Federation
11 Bedford Road
London
WC1R 4DX
UK
Phone: 44 171 242 6904
Fax: 44 171 405 7784

British Printing Society
Cobo
Beetons Avenue
Ash, Aldershot
Hampshire GU12 5DH
UK
Phone: 44 1252 26771

British Standards Institute
389 Chiswick High Road
London   W4 4AL
UK
Phone: 44 81 996 7021
Fax: 44 81 996 7048

Cooperative of Hellenic Screen Printers
150 Thessalonikis St.
11853 Athens
Greece
Phone: 30 1 3473376

Czech Association of the Graphic Arts Industry
Mikulandska 7
11361 Prague 1
Czech Republic
Phone: 42 2 249 15679
Fax: 42 2 2978 96

Danish Screen Printing Association
Norre Voldgade 34
DK-1358 Copenhagen K
Denmark
Phone: 45 33 151700

European Association of Engravers and Lithographers
Biebricher Alle 79
Postfach 1869
W-6200 Wiesbaden
Germany
Phone: 49 6121 803115
Fax: 49 6121 803113

European Committee of Associations of Printing and Paper Converting Machinery Manufacturers

via Bertoni 10
1-20154 Milan
Italy
Phone: 39 2 349 5144
Fax: 39 2 345 0647

European Rotogravure Association

Streitfeldstrasse 19
D-81673 Munich
Germany
Phone: 49 89 433010
Fax: 49 89 4362477

European Flexographic Technical Association

6 The Tynings
Clevedon, Avon BS217YP
UK
Phone: 44 0272 878090

Federation of Belgian Printing Industries

Belliardstraat 20 - Bte. 16
B-1040 Brussels
Belgium
Phone: 32 2 512 3638
Fax: 32 2 513 5676

Federation of European Publishers

92 Avenue de Tervuren
B-1040 Brussels
Belgium
Phone: 32 2 736 3616
Fax: 32 2 736 1987

Federation of European Screen Printing Associations

Association House
7a West Street
Relgate
Surrey RH2 9BL
UK
Phone: 44 1737 240788
Fax: 44 1737 240770

Federation of Master Printers in the Provinces of Denmark

Bogtrykernes Hus
DK-2100 Copenhagen
Denmark
Phone: 45 66 130604
Fax: 45 66 136115

Federation of Printing and Bookbinding Enterprises in Greece

22 Psaromiliggoi Street
Athens
Greece

Federation of Screenprinters of Luxembourg

BP 1604
L-1016
Luxembourg
Phone: 352 42 45111
Fax: 352 42 4525

Federation of Swiss Printing Industries

Schosshaldenstrasse 20
Postfach
CH-3000 Berne 32
Switzerland
Phone: 41 31 431511
Fax: 41 31 443738

Federation of the Associations of Technicians of the Paint, Varnish, Enamel, and Printing Ink Industries of Continental Europe
34 Chemin de Halage
La Bonneville
95540 Mary-sur-Oise
France
Phone: 33 1 48 675224

Finnish Printing Industry Federation
Lonnrtinkatu 11A
SF-00120 Helsinki
Finland
Phone: 358 022 877 200
Fax: 358 022 603 527

Finnish Pulp and Paper Research Institute
P.O. Box 70
SF-02151 Espoo 10
Finland
Phone: 358 0 43711
Fax: 358 0 464305

Finnish Screen Printing Association
Pl 174
SF-00141 Helsinki 14
Finland
Phone: 358 06221143

FOGRA (Graphic Technology Research Association of Germany)
Streitfeldstrasse 19
D-81675 Munich
Germany
Phone: 49 89 43182-0
Fax: 49 89 4316896

French Association of Bookbinders and Print Finishers
15 rue de Bussi
F-75006 Paris
France
Phone: 33 1 634 21 15
Fax: 33 1 40469112

French Association of Printing Companies and the Graphic Industries
11 Boulevard des Recollets
F-31078 Toulouse Cedex
France
Phone: 33 1 527592

French Federation of Gravure
3 rue Jules Cesar
F-75012 Paris
France
Phone: 33 1 43422700
Fax: 33 1 43411411

French National Association for the Coordination of Actions for the Formation of the Graphics Industries
263 rue de Paris
F-93514 Montreuil Cedex
France
Phone: 33 1 48518024

French National Association of Graphic Communication
8 rue de Berri
F-75008 Paris
France
Phone: 33 1 42250435
Fax: 33 1 42250432

French National Association of Graphic Designers
1 rue de Courcelles
F-75008 Paris
France
Phone: 33 1 47681994

French National Association of Gravure and Flexography
3 rue Sainte Elisabeth
F-75003 Paris
France
Phone: 33 1 42720808

French National Association of Offset and Lithographic Printers

36 rue des Bourdonnais
F-75001 Paris
France
Phone: 33 1 40 262508
Fax: 33 1 40 266551

French National Institute for the Graphic Arts Industries

296 rue de Charenton
F-75012 Paris
France
Phone: 33 1 345 5518

French Prepress Association

7 rue de Villersexel
F-75007 Paris
France
Phone: 33 1 45 494669
Fax: 33 1 45 449320

French Printing and Graphic Communication Association

115 Boulevard Saint Germain
F-75006 Paris
France
Phone: 33 1 44419040
Fax: 33 1 46337334

French Technical Association for the Development of Flexography

15 rue de l'Abbe Gregoire
F-75006 Paris
France
Phone: 33 1 45 44 13 37
Fax: 33 1 45 48 44 74

German Association of Lithography and Offset Printing

Rennweg 53
D-8500 Nuremberg
Germany
Phone: 49 911 551050

German Association of Printing Engineers

Lyoner Strasse 18
D-6000 Frankfurt 71
Germany
Phone: 49 69 6603454

German Association of Printing Ink Manufacturers

Karlstrasse 21
D-60329 Frankfurt/Main 1
Germany
Phone: 49 69 2556-1351
Fax: 49 69 253087

German Newspaper Research Institute

Haus der Bibliotheken
Wisstrasse 4
D-4600 Dortmund 1
Germany
Phone: 49 54 22 3216-20

German Printing Industry Federation

Biebricher Allee 79
Postfach 1869
D-65187 Wiesbaden
Germany
Phone: 49 611 8030
Fax: 49 611 803113

German Printing Industry Managers

Albert-Schweitzer-Strasse 7
D-6074 Rodermark
Germany
Phone: 49 6074 70545

German Professional Association of Printing and Papermaking

Rheinstrasse 6-8
Postfach 1489
D-6200 Wiesbaden
Germany
Phone: 49 6121 1311

German Research Association for Gravure Printing
Nobelstrasse 10
Stuttgart 80-Vaihingen
Germany
Phone: 49 685 28 51

German Union of Large Offset Businesses
Fritz Busche Gmbh
Kaiserstrasse 129
Postfach 1141
D-4600 Dortmund
Germany
Phone: 49 2 31 51801

Graphic Association of Denmark
Helgavej 26
DK-5100 Odense
Denmark
Phone: 45 66 130601
Fax: 45 66 136115

Graphic Technology Research Association (of Germany)
See FOGRA

Greater Paris Graphic Communication Association
46 rue de Berri
F-75008 Paris
France
Phone: 33 1 42 250435
Fax: 33 1 42 250432

Greek Lithographic Enterprises
Mitropoleos 12-14
10563 Athens
Greece
Phone: 30 1 322 0924

Guild of Graphic Industries of Barcelona Spain
Gran via de les Corts
Catalanes 645
Barcelona 10
Spain
Phone: 34 3 317 1008
Fax: 34 3 317 6229

Gutenberg Society International
Liebfrauenplatz 5
D-55116 Mainz
Germany
Phone: 49 6131 226420
Fax: 49 6131 123488

Hellenic Federation of Printing Industries
245 Syngrou Ave.
GR-17122 Athens
Greece
Phone: 30 1 93 00 440
Fax: 30 1 94 25 091

High Institute of the Printing Industry
Industrieweg 228
9030 Mariakerke
Belgium
Phone: 32 9 227 2625
Fax: 32 9 227 2642

Hungarian Technical Union of the Paper and Printing Industries
Fo utca 68
1027 Budapest
Postanschrift 433
1371 Budapest
Hungary
Phone: 361 201 8495
Fax: 361 202 0256

ICOGRADA Graphic Design Foundation

P.O. Box 398
London
W11 4UG
UK
Phone: 44 171 603 8494
Fax: 44 171 371 6040

IGT/Reprotest BV

Paper, Ink, and Graphic Arts Research
Postbus 94672
1090 GR Amsterdam
Netherlands
Phone: 31 20 6928988
Fax: 31 20 692 2710

Institute for Printing Machinery and Printing Processes

Darmstadt Technical College
D-6100 Darmstadt
Germany
Phone: 49 6151 162132
Fax: 49 6151 163632

Institute for Technology and Planning of Printing

Hochschule der Kunste
FB 5 - WE 2
Einsteinufer 43-53
D-1000 Berlin 10
Germany
Phone: 49 30 3185-0

Institute of Printing

8 Lonsdale Gardens
Tunbridge Wells
Kent TN1 1NU
UK
Phone: 44 1892 538118

Intergraf (International Confederation for Printing and Allied Industries)

18 Square Marie Louise
Bte. 25-27
B-1040 Brussels
Belgium
Phone: 32 2 230 2672
Fax: 32 2 231 1464

International Association for Newspaper and Media Technology

Washingtonplatz 1
D-64287 Darmstadt
Germany
Phone: 49 6151 70050
Fax: 49 6151 700572

International Association of Research Institutes for the Graphic Arts Industry

18 The Ridgeway
Fetcham Park
Leatherhead Surrey KT22 9AZ
Phone:
Fax:

International Color Consortium

WWW: http://www.color.org/

International Federation of Newspaper Publishers

25 rue d'Astorg
F-75008 Paris
France
Fax: 33 1 45230663

International Graphical Alliance

Sonnhaldenstrasse 3
CH-8032 Zurich
Switzerland
Phone: 41 1 2525042

International Graphical Federation

Monbijoustrasse 73
CH-3007 Berne
Switzerland
Phone: 41 31 459920

International Typographical Association

Kattowitzer Strasse 57
D-6230 Frankfurt am Main 80
Germany

Irish Master Printers Association

33 Parkgate Street
Dublin
Ireland
Phone: 353 1 867 9679

Irish Printing Federation

Baggot Bridge House
84-86 Lower Baggot Street
Dublin 2
Ireland
Phone: 353 1 660 1011
Fax: 353 1 660 1717

Italian Association for the Printing, Paper, and Board Converting Industries

Piazaa della Conciliazione 1
1-20123 Milan
Italy
Phone: 39 2 498 1051
Fax: 39 2 481 6947

Italian Association of Printing Ink Manufacturers

via Accademia 33
1-20131 Milan
Italy
Phone: 39 2 63621

Italian Graphics Cultural Association

via Morgari 36/B
I-10125 Turin
Italy
Phone: 39 11 669 0577
Fax: 39 11 668 9200

Italian Technical Association for the Development of Flexography

Via Sandro Botticelli 19
1-20133 Milan
Italy
Phone: 39 2 236 4557

National Central Committee for the German Printing Industry

Kurfurstenanlage 69
D-6900 Heidelberg 1
Germany
Phone: 49 6221 21600

Norwegian Federation of Graphic Enterprises

Havanelageret
Langkaia 1
N-0150 Oslo
Norway
Phone: 47 22 41 21 80
Fax: 47 22 39 69 72

Norwegian Institute for the Graphic Arts Industries

Forskningsparken
Gaustadallen 21
N-0137 Oslo
Norway
Phone: 47 22 958550
Fax: 47 22 602818

Norwegian Screen Printing Association

Apotekergt 18
N-3190 Horten
Norway
Phone: 47 33 45 945

Paper Federation of Great Britain

Papermakers House
Rivenhall Road
Westlea
Swindon SN5 7BE
UK
Phone: 44 1793 886086
Fax: 44 1793 886182

PIRA International

(Printing Industry Research Association)
Randalls Rd.
Surrey Leatherhead KT22 7RU
UK
Phone: 44 13 723 76161
Fax: 44 13 723 77526

Portuguese Printing and Converting Association

Largo do Casal Vistoso
No 2/D - Escritorios B C D
P-1900 Lisbon
351 1 849 1020
Fax: 351 1 847 0778

Printing Historical Society

St. Bride Printing Library
Bride Lane
Fleet Street
London EC4Y 8EE
UK
Phone: 44 171 353 4660
Fax: 44 171 583 7073

Professional Confederation of Hungarian Printers

Eotvos U. 12
H-1067 Budapest
Hungary
Phone: 361 268 1460
Fax: 361 268 1462

Royal Dutch Association of Printing and Allied Industries

Startbaan 10
Postbus 220
1180 AE Amstelveen
Netherlands
Phone: 31 20 547 5678
Fax: 31 20 547 5475

Scandinavian Paint and Printing Ink Research Institute

Agern Alle 3
DK-2970 Horsholm
Denmark
Phone: 45 47 2 57 03 55

Scottish Print Employers Federation

48 Palmerston Place
Edinburgh
EH12 5DE
UK
Phone: 44 1 31 220 4353
Fax: 44 1 31 220 4344

Screen Printing Association of the UK

Association House
7a West Street
Reigate
Surry RH2 9BL
Phone: 44 1737 240792
Fax: 44 1737 240770

Society of Typographic Designers

Wellington House
Church Road
Ashford Kent TN 24 1PE
UK
Phone: 44 0243 24618

Spanish Association for the Development of the Graphic Arts

Jesus Maestro s/n
Madrid 3
Spain
Phone: 34 234 5359

Spanish Association of Manufacturers of Printing Inks
Lauria 44-7 - 1a
E-06009 Barcelona
Spain
Phone: 34 93 318 9097

Spanish Association of the Graphic Arts
Plaza de Espana s/n
E-08004 Barcelona
Spain
Phone: 34 3 423 3101
Fax: 34 3 426 1056

Spanish National Federation of the Graphics Industry
Barquillo 11, 4oD
E Madrid 4
Spain
Phone: 34 1 522 90 84
Fax: 34 1 532 67 45

Spanish Screen Printing Association
Vilgeliu 16
3 planta
Barcelona 4
Spain
Phone: 34 931 371 3106

Standing Conference of Institutions of Printing Education
Barking College
Dagenham Road
Romford
Essex RM7 0XU
Phone: 44 1708 766841

Swedish Graphic Arts Research Laboratory
Box 5637
S-11486 Stockholm
Sweden
Phone: 46 8 453 5700
Fax: 46 8 453 5757

Swedish Graphic Companies' Federation
Box 16 383
S-10327 Stockholm
Sweden
Phone: 46 8 762 6800
Fax: 46 8 453 5757

Swedish Graphic Reproduction Federation
Sankt Erisgaten 26 11
Box 12069
Stockholm S-10222
Sweden

Swedish Printing Industries Federation
Sankt Erisgaten 26 11
Box 12069
Stockholm S-10222
Sweden

Swedish Screen Printing Association
Sankt Erisgaten 26 11
Box 12069
Stockholm S-10222
Sweden

Swiss Association of Bookbinding
Monbijoustrasse 14
Postfach 5236
CH-3001 Berne
Switzerland
Phone: 41 31 261 587
Fax: 41 31 260715

Swiss Association of Printing Ink Manufacturers
Neugasse 6
CH-8005 Zurich
Switzerland
Phone: 41 1 271 5151
Fax: 41 1 271 7288

Swissgraphic

Schosshaldenstrasse 20
CH-3000 Bern 32
Switzerland
Phone: 41 31 4311515
Fax: 41 31 343738

Swiss Graphic Arts Association

Carmenstrasse 6
Postfach 39
CH-8030 Zurich 30
Switzerland
Phone: 41 1 252 1440
Fax: 41 1 252 1743

Swiss Graphic Designers

Limmatstrasse 63
CH-8005 Zurich
Switzerland
Phone: 41 1 272 4555
Fax: 41 1 272 5282

Swiss Gravure Association

Goliathgasse 37
CH-9000 St. Gallen
Switzerland
Phone: 41 71 240591
Fax: 41 71 251955

Swiss Screen Printing Association

P.O. 284
CH-1800 Vevey
Switzerland
Phone: 41 37 301944

Technical Association of the Italian Graphic Arts

Via Sandro Botticelli 19
1-20133 Milan
Italy
Phone: 39 2 236 4558

Technical Working Group of Offset Plate Manufacturers

Postfach 5606
D-6200 Wiesbaden
Germany
Phone: 49 6121 688247
Fax: 49 6121 600734

UGRA (Association for the Promotion of Research in the Graphic Arts Industry)

c/o EMPA
Unterstrabe 11
CH-9001 St. Gallen
Switzerland
Phone: 41 7 120 9141
Fax: 41 7 122 7220

Vienna Guild of Gravure and Metal Printers

Salesiangergasse 1
A-1030 Vienna
Austria
Phone: 43 725 611

Web Offset Newspaper Association

Advanced Technology Group
74-77 Great Russell Street
London WC1B 3DA
UK
Phone: 44 171 636 7014
Fax: 44 171 631 4119

Suggested Readings: Extra Credit

Want to get a head start on your competition? The following is a list of books and magazines that offer in-depth information about the graphic communications field and printing processes.

Books

Agfa Digital Color Prepress, Vols. 1-2, et. al. Mount Prospect, IL: Agfa Prepress Education Resources, 1990, 1992, etc.

Color and Its Reproduction, 2nd edition, revised. Field, Gary G. Pittsburgh: Graphic Arts Technical Foundation, 1998.

Creating Your Career in Communications and Entertainment, Mogel, Leonard. Pittsburgh: Graphic Arts Technical Foundation, 1998.

Flexography Primer, 2nd edition. Crouch, J. Page. Pittsburgh: Graphic Arts Technical Foundation, 1998.

The GATF Encyclopedia of Graphic Communications. Romano, Frank and Romano, Richard. Pittsburgh: Graphic Arts Technical Foundation, 1998.

Getting It Printed. Beach, Mark. Cincinnati: North Light Books, 1993.

Glossary of Graphic Communications, 3rd edition. Groff, Pamela. Pittsburgh: Graphic Arts Technical Foundation, 1997.

Graphic Communications Trade Customs/Business Practices. Sponsored by the Graphic Arts Technical Foundation, the National Association of Printers and Lithographers, and the Printing Industries of America. Published in 1994.

Graphically Speaking. Beach, Mark. Manzanita, OR: Coast to Coast, 1992.

Gravure Primer. Kasunich, Cheryl. Pittsburgh: Graphic Arts Technical Foundation, 1998.

Guide to Desktop Publishing, 2nd edition. Cavuoto, James and Beale, Steven. Pittsburgh: Graphic Arts Technical Foundation, 1995.

Handbook of Printing Processes. Stevenson, Deborah L. Pittsburgh: Graphic Arts Technical Foundation, 1994.

Lithographers Manual, 9th edition. Destree, Thomas, editor. Pittsburgh: Graphic Arts Technical Foundation, 1994.

Lithography Primer, 2nd edition. Wilson, Daniel G. Pittsburgh: Graphic Arts Technical Foundation, 1997.

Looking Good in Print. Parker, Roger C. Research Triangle Park, NC: Ventana Communications Group, Inc., 1996.

On-Demand Printing, 2nd edition. Fenton, Howard M. and Romano, Frank J. Pittsburgh: Graphic Arts Technical Foundation, 1997.

Printing Technology. Adams, J. Michael; Faux, David; and Rieber, Lloyd J. Albany, NY: Delmar, 1996.

Pocket Guide to Digital Prepress. Romano, Frank J. Albany, NY: Delmar Publishers, 1996.

Pocket Pal, 16th edition. Bruno, M., editor Nashville, TN: International Paper Print Resource Group, Inc., 1995.

Professional Print Buying. Green, Phil, editor. Pittsburgh: Graphic Arts Technical Foundation/Pira International, 1997.

Screen Printing Primer. 2nd Ingram, Samuel T. Pittsburgh: Graphic Arts Technical Foundation, 1998.

Technovation Handbook: A Review of Current Imaging Technologies Affecting Major Print Markets, 2nd edition. Menasha, WI: Banta Corporation, 1996.

Understanding Digital Color. Green, Phil. Pittsburgh: Graphic Arts Technical Foundation, 1995.

Understanding Digital Imposition. Hinderliter, Hal. Pittsburgh: Graphic Arts Technical Foundation, 1998.

Understanding Electronic Communications: Printing in the Information Age. Ajayi, A'isha and Groff, Pamela. Pittsburgh: Graphic Arts Technical Foundation, 1997.

Periodicals

American Ink Maker—(Monthly) Magazine serving ink, color, and allied industries

American Printer—(Monthly) The graphic arts management magazine

Converting—(Monthly) For printers printer on paperboard

Digital Production Executive [formerly PRE]—(Monthly) For production executives using digital technology

Editor and Publisher—(Weekly) The independent weekly journal of the newspaper industry

Electronic Publishing—(Monthly) Covers digital equipment for business

Flexo—(Monthly) For flexographic printers

Folio—(Monthly) The magazine for magazine management

GATFWorld—(Bimonthly) Magazine of the Graphic Arts Technical Foundation

Graphic Arts Monthly—(Monthly) For print production and plant managers

Gravure—(Quarterly) The magazine for gravure printers

High Volume Printer—(Monthly) For managers in large printing plants

New Media—(Monthly) For creative professionals in the digital field

Package Printing and Converting—(Monthly) Magazine for producers of labels, tabs, flexible packaging, folding cartons, and diecut items

Prepress Bulletin—(Monthly) Technical publication of the International Prepress Association

Presstime—(Monthly) The magazine of the Newspaper Association of America

Print On-Demand Business—(Bimonthly) Magazine of digital printing and document management

Printing Impressions—(Monthly) Magazine for commercial printers

Printing News—(Weekly) The newsweekly covering trends from imaging to finishing

Publish—(Monthly) The magazine for electronic publishing professionals

Publishers Weekly—(Weekly) Magazine of the book trade

Publishing & Production Executive—(Monthly) Magazine for buyers of printing, prepress, paper, and publishing systems for the printing of magazines, catalog, book, agency, and corporate communications

Quick Print—(Monthly) The magazine for small commercial print shops and copy shops

Screen Printing—(Monthly) Magazine for screen printers

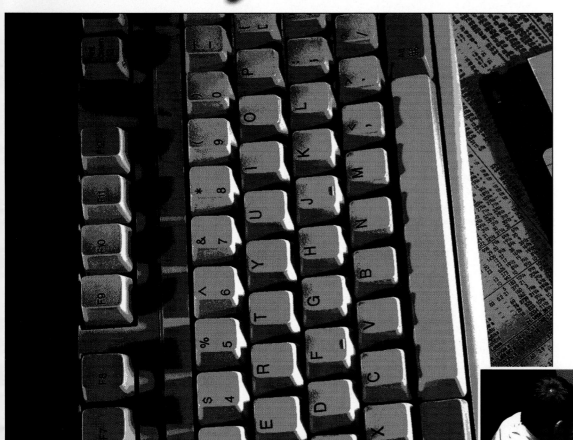

Glossary:
Coming to Terms

From airbrush to zooming, printers have developed their own ways to describe some of what happens in production. You may want to use the following glossary to look up unfamiliar terms. Or you might use it as a mini-education, a compact way to learn more about the printing process.

access. To retrieve data from a hard drive or other physical storage medium or another computer connected via network or modem.

accordion fold. Two or more folds parallel to each other with adjacent folds in opposite directions, resembling the bellows of an accordion. Alternative term: fanfold.

acid. (1) In lithography, a dampening solution ingredient that enables gum arabic to cling to the nonimage areas of the plate. (2) Perchloride of iron used to etch gravure cylinders. Alternative term: etchant.

active-matrix display. A full-color liquid-crystal display that offers higher resolution, contrast, and vertical refresh rate than a passive-matrix display.

additive color process. Mixing red, green, and blue lights in various combinations to create a color reproduction or image. A color television system is an example of the additive color process.

additive primaries. Highly saturated red, green, and blue lights that, when mixed together in varying combinations and intensities, can produce any other color.

additives/modifiers. Ingredients added to a printing ink to give it special characteristics or properties. Modifiers promote adhesion and film flexibility, provide abrasion resistance and slip, and serve as antiblocking and antipinholing compounds.

adhesive binding. Applying a glue or another, usually hot-melt, substance along the backbone edges of assembled, printed sheets.

adjacency effect. The property of the eye that causes the same color to look different when surrounded by or adjacent to other colors. A color will appear darker when surrounded by a lighter color, or lighter when surrounded by a darker color.

Adobe Acrobat. One popular portable document file (PDF) format. Through Acrobat or another PDF, users can read electronic versions of printed documents that maintain the attributes (bold and italic type and other formatting choices) assigned to a printed original.

airbrush. (1) A miniature, pencil-shaped hand sprayer used to retouch drawings, photographs, and density values on continuous-tone negatives. (2) Adding or removing process color values in a designated picture area displayed on the screen of an electronic color imaging system. The operator airbrushes the image by using a mouse or guiding a stylus on a digitizing tablet and adjusting the strength and width of the electronic "spray."

alcohol. (1) One of a family of organic solvents used in flexographic and gravure inks. (2) An organic substance added to the dampening solution of a lithographic printing press to reduce the surface tension of water. Alcohol makes the dampening solution more uniform, allowing for a thinner application of solution to the plate.

alcohol substitutes. Chemicals used in lithographic dampening solution in place of isopropyl alcohol.

analog device. A computer or other device that uses continuous signals of varying intensity rather than digital signals that can only be "on" or "off." Some color scanners use hard-wired electronic circuits to perform analog color correction and tone reproduction, while other scanners use digital data to perform similar functions.

apron. A blank space at the edge of a foldout that permits the sheet to be folded and tipped in the finishing process without marring the copy.

art. (1) Hand-drawn originals used for photo-mechanical reproduction. (2) Flat graphic images that are reproduced in the printing process. Some examples include paintings, photographs, and computer-generated diagrams and charts.

artwork. A general term for photographs, drawings, paintings, and other materials prepared to illustrate printed matter.

artwork, comprehensive. Design produced primarily to give the customer an approximate idea of what the printed piece will look like. Alternative terms: comprehensive; comp.

artwork, separated. Design that indicates each area to print in a color on a different layout.

assembling. Collecting individual sheets or signatures into a complete set with pages in proper sequence and alignment. Assembling is followed by binding.

assembly. Placing film elements together in order on a suitable substrate.

authoring. In multimedia, the complete process of preparing a presentation, including writing and creating the sound, graphic, and video components.

author's alterations (AA). Changes requested by the author or author's representative after the original copy has been paginated. Alternative term: author's corrections.

back pressure. The force between the blanket cylinder and the impression cylinder that facilitates the transfer of the image from the blanket to the printing substrate. Alternative term: impression pressure.

background. The area of an illustration or photograph that appears behind the principal subject.

backing away (from the ink fountain). A condition in which an ink does not flow under its own weight or remain in contact with the fountain roller. It "backs away" and is not transferred to the ductor roller. Eventually, the prints become uneven, streaky, and weak.

A conical ink agitator, which applies a finite amount of force to the ink, keeps it flowing or prevents it from backing up in the fountain while automatic ink leveling keeps the fountain full.

backlighting. (1) Light shining on the subject from the direction opposite the camera, as distinguished from frontlighting and sidelighting. (2) The process of illuminating transparent artwork or screen-printed transparency films from behind. (3) Illuminating transparent or translucent copy from behind on a graphic arts camera.

backup registration. Correct relative position of the printing on one side of the sheet or web and the printing on the other side.

balance. Placement of colors, light and dark masses, or large and small objects in a picture or layout to create harmony and equilibrium.

base. (1) The single coloring, pigment, or dye dispersed in an ink vehicle. The bases commonly used to manufacture offset inks are aluminum hydrate and a gloss white. (2) A flat sheet of paper or film that provides the support for a photosensitive coating or emulsion. (3) A modifying additive for screen printing inks. (4) The initial artwork or pasteup board to which all overlays are attached.

basis weight. The weight in pounds of a ream (500 sheets) of paper cut to its basic size in inches. Some basic sizes include 25×38 in. for book papers, 20×26 in. for cover papers, 22½×28½ in. or 22½×35 in. for bristol, and 25½×30½ in. for index. For example, 500 sheets of 25×38-in., 80-lb. coated paper will weigh eighty pounds.

bayonet. On a saddle stitcher, the prong onto which the signature drops just before it is picked up by the chain pin. Alternative term: sword.

bearer. A hardened steel ring located at the end of the plate and blanket cylinders on a lithographic press. The bearers are the true diameter of the cylinders. When the cylinders are in contact during printing, the bearers are forced together under preset pressure.

bearer pressure. The force with which the bearers of opposed cylinders contact each other on an offset lithographic press.

bed. On a guillotine paper cutter, the flat metal surface on which the cutting is performed.

binary digit (bit). The most basic unit of information in the binary numbering system. Binary information is stored as a series of zeros and ones, indicating low (off) or high (on) electrical current.

bind. To join the pages of a book together with thread, wire, adhesive, crash (a coarse fabric), or other materials, or enclose them in a cover.

binder. (1) The adhesive components of an ink that hold the pigment to the printed surface. (2) In paper, an adhesive component used to cement inert filler, such as clay, to the sheet. (3) Carriers or vehicles that fix the pigments in screen printing dyes onto the fibers of the fabric being decorated. (4) A person or machine that binds books. (5) A cover designed to hold loose pages and/or pamphlets, e.g., three-ring and post-style binders.

binder's creep. The slight but cumulative extension of the edges of each inserted spread or signature beyond the edges of the signature that encloses it. This results in progressively smaller trim size on the inside pages. Alternative terms: pushout; shingling.

bindery. A facility where finishing operations such as folding, joining signatures, and covering are performed.

binding. Joining the assembled pages of a printed piece together. Binding takes many forms including saddle-stitching, adhesive binding, mechanical binding, loose-leaf binding, and Smyth sewing. It is also used as a generic term to describe all finishing operations.

binding dummy. Blank pages of assembled signatures stitched and trimmed to show the amount of compensation needed for creep.

bit. The smallest unit of information used in a computer file. It has one of two possible values—zero or one—used to indicate "on" or "off" or "yes" or "no" in the storage and transfer of electronic information and images.

bitmap. An image represented by an array of picture elements, each of which is encoded as a single binary digit. Alternative term: bit image.

black. (1) The absence of all reflected light; the absence of color. (2) An ink that appears to absorb all wavelengths of light. It is used as one ink in the four-color printing process.

black printer. (1) The plate that prints black ink in four-color process printing. (2) The halftone film used to burn the plate that will print black ink or the printing screen used in process-color reproduction to print the color black and add detail to the print. The letter "K" is often used to designate this color.

black-and-white (B/W, B&W). Originals and printed material comprised only of black and white with tones of gray.

black-and-white art. Line art usually produced on smooth or textured board with pen or brush and black ink or generated using a computer.

blank. (1) A thick paperboard, coated or uncoated, produced on a cylinder machine and designed for printing. Thickness ranges from 15 to 48 points (0.380 to 1.220 millimeters). (2) An unprinted page or sheet side. (3) Unprinted cardboard, metal sheets, or other substrates used for making displays and signs.

blanket. (1) In presswork, a sheet of cork, felt, or rubber used on a press platen or impression cylinder to cushion the impression in printing. (2) In lithography, a rubber-coated fabric mounted on a cylinder that receives the inked impression from the plate and transfers (or offsets) it to the paper. Such blankets are also mounted on the impression cylinders of sheetfed gravure presses.

blanket cylinder. The cylinder that carries the offset rubber blanket, placing it in contact with the inked image on the plate cylinder and then transferring the inked image to the paper carried by the impression cylinder. The blanket cylinder has a gap where the blanket clamps are located. The outer ends of the cylinder house the bearers.

blanket piling. Piling develops when poorly bonded paper surface fibers, coating from coated paper, or slitter dust accumulates on the blanket surface. It may occur in the image and nonimage areas. A large degree of piling can distort the ink transfer, leading to poor print quality.

blanket smash. Areas of low ink density in the press sheet image. The caliper of the blanket in these areas is too low to develop sufficient impression pressure against the plate or paper or both. Alternative term: blanket low spots.

blanket-to-blanket. A cylinder configuration on a perfecting press whereby two blanket cylinders, each acting as an impression cylinder for the other, simultaneously print on both sides of the paper passing between them. Most commonly used in web press designs. Alternative term: perfecting press.

bleed. (1) A printing area that extends to the edge of the sheet or page after it is trimmed. (2) A slight extension or thickening of printing detail, usually of the lighter color or tint, to produce color overlap zones, so that a white gap will not show in printing when slight variations in register occur throughout the pressrun. (3) Condition that results when a solvent causes a pigment color to spread or run.

blend. Joining two colors so smoothly that there is no perceptible line at the intersection. In digital painting, the quality of the blending process is an indication of the quality of the electronic prepress system.

blueline. A blue-on-white print made by exposing sensitized paper to a negative in contact. It is used as a final proof before platemaking in film-based reproduction systems.

blur. In electronic prepress, softening the detail of an image feature. The reverse process is known as sharpening.

board. A heavy, thick sheet of paper or other fibrous substance, usually with a thickness greater than 6 mil (0.006 inch).

brightness. (1)The subjective perception of luminous intensity from any light sensation, running the gamut from lightness and brilliance to dimness or darkness. (2) With paper, the percent reflectance of blue light only, centering on the wavelength of 457 nm.

byte. A single group of bits (most often eight) that are processed as a unit. Also the smallest addressable unit of main storage in a computer system.

calendering. (1) A method of producing a very high gloss surface on paper stock by passing the sheet between a series of rollers under pressure. (2) A process for smoothing paper by running it between polished metal rollers.

calibrate. To adjust the scale on a measuring instrument such as a densitometer to a standard for specific conditions.

calibration. A process by which a scanner, monitor, or output device is adjusted to provide a more accurate display and reproduction of images.

calibration bars. On a negative, proof, or printed piece, a strip of tones used to check printing quality.

California job case. An open box with compartments in which individual type characters are separated for the hand compositor.

caliper. The thickness of a sheet of paper or other material measured under specific conditions. Caliper is usually expressed in mils or points, both ways of expressing thousandths of an inch.

callout. A portion of text, usually duplicated from accompanying text, enlarged, and set off in quotes and/or a box to draw attention to what surrounds it.

camera. A light-tight photographic device that records the image of an object formed when light rays pass through a lens and fall on a flat, photosensitive surface. In addition to the lens, other camera components include automatic or manual focus and size adjustments, a film- or paper-holding mechanism, and an area for previewing the final image. A light source and metering device may also be included.

camera, digital. A photographic system using a charged-coupled device to transform visual information into pixels that are assigned binary codes so that they can be manipulated, compressed, stored, or transmitted as electronic files.

camera, process. A camera designed especially to create halftone images and color separations for photomechanical reproduction and similar work.

camera exposure. Producing a latent image on photosensitive material from the light rays that a subject reflects or transmits when photographed under controlled conditions of time and intensity.

camera-ready copy. All printing elements (fully paginated text and illustrations) as prepared for final reproduction. Prior to the advent of electronic prepress, a graphic arts camera was used to photograph art and copy that had been pasted-up manually to an art board. Now the term camera-ready copy can be used to refer to digital computer output (such as an advertisement, resume, or other small job) that requires little or no preparation by the printer prior to duplication.

case. (1) In typography, a portioned receptacle or tray used to store type and other hand-composition materials. The California job case is a well-known example. (2) In bookbinding, inserting and attaching a book into prepared (hard) covers.

casebound book. A book bound with a stiff, hard cover. Alternative term: hardbound book.

cathode-ray tube (CRT). An electronic vacuum tube containing a heated cathode that generates electrons and multiple grids for accelerating the electrons to a flat screen at the end of the tube. The screen coating fluoresces wherever the electrons strike it, giving off light. CRTs are used as monitors in video display terminals (VDTs).

CCD array. A group of light-sensitive recording elements often arranged in a line (linear array) and used as a scanner image-sensing device. See also: charge-coupled device.

CD-ROM (compact disk—read-only memory). An optical data storage device that consists of a platter in which data is etched as a series of pits and lands (the space between the pits) in a continuous spiral. Derived from the compact audio disk (CD), a typical CD-ROM holds 650 MB of digitally encoded computer data, which the user can retrieve (but not alter) using a laser-based reader.

center spread. Facing pages in the center of a newspaper section or a signature.

chalking. Poor adhesion of ink to printing surface. This condition results when the substrate absorbs the ink vehicle too rapidly. The ink dries slowly and rubs off as a dusty powder.

charge-coupled device. A component of an electronic scanner or camera that digitizes images. A CCD consists of a set of image-sensing elements (photosites) arranged in a linear or area array. Images are digitized by an external light source that illuminates the source document, which reflects the light through optics onto the silicon light sensors in the array. This generates electrical signals in each photosite proportional to the intensity of the illumination.

chill rolls. On a web offset press, the section located after the drying oven where heatset inks are cooled below their setting temperature.

cleanup. (1) Washing a lithographic plate during the pressrun to make the nonimage areas ink repellent again. (2) After a pressrun, removing the plates and washing the entire press and surrounding area. Alternative term: washup.

clip art. Previously developed designs and graphics used in composing new artwork. Most clip art, which can be purchased on CDs, online, or in booklets, is in the public domain (copyright free) and can be used over and over again by anyone for any purpose once the initial purchase is made. Other clip art is purchased on a fee-per-usage basis.

cloning. A retouching function available on a color imaging system. It is normally used to remove image defects by replacing pixels in the defective areas with duplicate pixels from adjacent, nondefective areas. It can also be used to duplicate sections of an image. Alternative term: pixel swopping.

close register. Term used to describe jobs with smaller register tolerances. Alternative term: tight register.

clothbound. A casebound book with a fabric cover.

coating. (1) An unbroken, clear film applied to a substrate in layers to protect and seal it, or to make it glossy. (2) Applying waxes, adhesives, varnishes, or other protective or sealable chemicals to a substrate during the converting process. (3) The mineral substances (clay, blanc fixe, satin white, etc.) applied to the surface of a paper or board. (4) In photography and photomechanics, applying varnishes and other mixtures to plates and negatives; or applying light-sensitive solutions to plate surfaces.

collate. The process of sorting the pages of a publication in the proper order.

colophon. (1) Traditionally, the printer's signature and the date of completion written at the beginning or end of a book. (2) The publisher's trademark printed on cover or title page. (3) A modern colophon at the back of book often includes information about the paper, typeface, and typesetting method used, how the illustrations were produced, and what printing process was employed.

color. A visual sensation produced in the brain when the eye views various wavelengths of light. Color viewing is a highly subjective experience that varies from individual to individual. In the graphic arts industry, lighting standards and color charts help ensure the accuracy of color reproduction.

color, HiFi. A special (high-fidelity) color reproduction process based on a model that uses seven basic colors instead of four to expand the color gamut of the printing process. The basic colors are cyan, yellow, magenta, orange, green, violet, and black. Color separations are made with stochastic screening technology to prevent the formation of moiré patterns, which would occur if conventional halftone screening technology was used.

color balance. (1) The correct combination of cyan, magenta, and yellow needed to reproduce a specific photograph without an unwanted color cast or color bias. (2) The specific combination of yellow, magenta, and cyan needed to produce a neutral gray in the color separation process. (3) The ability of a film to reproduce the colors in an original scene. Color films are balanced during manufacture to compensate for exposure to specific light sources.

color bar. A device printed in a trim area of a press sheet to monitor printing variables such as trapping, ink density, dot gain, and print contrast. It usually consists of overprints of two- and three-color solids and tints; solid and tint blocks of cyan, magenta, yellow, and black; and additional aids such as resolution targets and dot gain scales.

color blindness. A deficiency in vision that permits a person to see only two hues in the spectrum, usually yellow and blue.

color cast. Modifying a hue by adding a trace of another hue to create such combinations as yellowish green or pinkish blue. Color casts can be undesirable as in the contamination of the desired hue by a second hue. For example, a gray intended to appear as a neutral can under some conditions have a red, yellow, or blue cast or appearance. Other colors can have a cast as well, e.g., reds with a yellow or blue cast or blues with a red or yellow cast, etc.

color computer. The analog or digital device in the color scanner that determines the amount of each process ink necessary to reproduce the color in the original image. A digital color computer uses lookup tables to determine the dot percentages, while an analog color computer typically uses masking equations to determine the percentages.

color correction. (1) A photographic, electronic, or manual procedure used to compensate for the deficiencies of the process inks and color separation. (2) Any color alteration requested by a customer.

color electronic prepress system. Originally, a special computer dedicated to image manipulation and page-makeup in the graphic arts production environment. These machines replaced the manual correction techniques previously accomplished with duplicate transparencies and emulsion stripping. Today, personal computers and application software are frequently used to complete many CEPS functions.

color fidelity. How well a printed piece matches the original.

color gamut. The range colors that can be formed by all possible combinations of the colorants in a color reproduction system.

color management system. An electronic prepress tool that provides a way to correlate the color-rendering capabilities of input devices (e.g., scanners and digital cameras), color monitors, and output devices (e.g., digital color proofers, imagesetters, and color printers) to produce predictable, consistent color. Color management consists of three primary steps: (1) calibration of input devices, monitors, and output devices to known specifications, (2) characterization, which is a way of determining the color "profile" of a particular device, and (3) conversion, which performs the "color correction" function between color-imaging devices.

color primaries, additive. The three basic colors, which, when properly selected and mixed, produce any hue. In the visual spectrum, the three primary colors are green, red, and blue. When combined, these colors form white light. In the printing process, the three primary (process) colors are yellow, magenta, and cyan.

color scanner. A device incorporating a digital or analog computer that separates colored originals electronically by using the three additive primary colors of light in the form of blue, green, and red filters, plus a preprogrammed black printer correctly balanced with the color separations. A light beam moves over the image point by point, generating a separate, color-corrected, continuous-tone intermediate or screened halftone film negative or positive representing each of the process colors and black.

color separation. Using red, green, and blue filters to divide the colors of a multicolored original into the three process colors and black. The four resulting film intermediates are used to prepare the yellow, magenta, cyan, and black printing plates.

color sequence. The order in which colors are printed on a substrate as indicated by the order in which the inks are supplied to the printing units on the press. Color sequence determines how well the inks will trap on the substrate. Alternative term: color rotation.

color temperature. The degree (expressed in Kelvins) to which a blackbody must be heated to produce a certain color radiation. For example, 5,000 Kelvin is the graphic arts viewing standard.

color transparency. A positive color photographic image on a clear film base. It must be viewed by transmitted light.

colorimeter. An instrument that measures and compares the hue, purity, and brightness of colors in a manner that simulates how people perceive color.

colorimetry. The science of determining and specifying colors.

column inch. A unit of measurement that is one inch deep and one column wide.

comb, plastic binding. A curved or rake-shaped plastic strip inserted through slots punched along the binding edge of the sheet.

command-line interface (CLI). Use of keyboarded instructions rather than a mouse and graphical elements to direct computer operations.

common-impression cylinder (CIC). A cylinder configuration used in both web and sheetfed press designs. The common impression cylinder is in contact with several blanket cylinders that are, in turn, in contact with plate cylinders. This configuration is used to print more than one color on one side of the sheet or web, in one printing unit. The CIC configuration saves space and reduces the chance of doubling.

common-impression press. A flexo or sheetfed or web offset press that has one large-drum impression cylinder, which holds or supports the substrate, and several color stations positioned around it.

complementary colors. Any two opposite (or contrasting) colors that produce white or gray when combined. In printing, complementary colors neutralize or accentuate each other, diminishing or enhancing the attention value on the print.

composing. The process of setting type.

composite. A single film carrying two or more images (usually line, halftone, or screen tint) as a result of photocombining (contacting) two or more separate film images.

composition. (1) Setting or assembling type. (2) Formatting typeset text before printing. Alternative terms: pagination and page makeup.

computer graphics. The process of integrating text and art and completing page layout on a computer before outputting it to a laser printer or imagesetter.

conductivity. The measurement of a solution's ability to conduct electricity, based on its concentration of ions. The measurement is expressed in microohms. Conductivity is the most accurate method of measuring fountain solution concentration in lithography due to the increased use of buffering agents to control pH levels.

cones. The sensors in the eye that permit color vision.

configuration. A group of machines that are inter-connected and programmed to operate as a system.

console. The computer system workstation where operators perform specific tasks by executing commands through a keyboard. Modern presses have consoles that control inking, dampening, and plate register moves. The results of the operator's commands can be reviewed on a nearby monitor.

contact film. Blue-sensitive, continuous-tone film with a relatively high maximum density, excellent resolution, and a special antihalation backing that allows exposure through its base without loss in quality. This film has been designed specifically to reproduce a same-size reverse (positive) image from an original negative, or a negative image from a film positive as the films are held together in a vacuum frame. Darkroom (high-speed) contact films may be handled under red or yellow safelights while roomlight (slow-speed) films may be handled under yellow fluorescent or subdued white lighting. Alternative term: color-blind film.

contact printing. Producing a photographic print by exposing sensitized paper, film, or printing plates held against a negative or positive in a vacuum frame. The resulting contact print is a same-size negative or positive reproduction.

continuous feeder. A paper-supply mechanism that can be reloaded without stopping the press.

continuous form. A series of connected sheets that feed sequentially through a printing device.

continuous tone. A photographic image or artwork that has not been screened. It has infinite tone gradations between the lightest highlights and the deepest shadows.

Glossary

continuous-tone negative. An inverse impression of tones from the original reproduced on sensitized film without using a halftone contact screen.

continuous-tone proof. An illustration without halftone dots, which is produced on a computer screen at view-file or fine-file resolutions with the red, green, blue (RGB) color parameters.

contrast. The relationship or degree of tonal gradation between the lightest and darkest (highlight and shadow) areas in an original, reproduction, or negative.

converting. Any manufacturing or finishing operation completed after printing to form the printed item into the final product. Bagmaking, coating, waxing, laminating, folding, slitting, gluing, box manufacture, and diecutting are some examples. Converting units may be attached to the end of the press, or the operation may be handled by a special outside facility.

copier. A machine that makes reproductions directly from graphic materials by the electrophotographic (xerographic) process or another nonimpact method.

copy. (1) Any material given to the printer for reproduction, particularly text and artwork. (2) To duplicate a photograph by contact printing.

copy, hard. Printed machine output of a photographic proof or text.

copy, soft. Text or images viewed or previewed on a computer monitor.

copy preparation. Specifying the size and location of type and illustrations and positioning them properly on a page.

copyfitting. Adjusting copy to the allotted space, by editing the text or changing the type size and leading.

corrugated board. A laminate made from flat sheets of paper and paper stock with a fluted, ridged, or grooved surface.

covering. The process of pasting endpapers to a hardback book and drying them under pressure.

creasing. (1) Pressing lines into a book cover during binding. (2) Crimping or indenting along the binding edge of sheets or pages so that they will lie flat and bend easily. (3) Indenting bristol or boxboard to guide subsequent folding or forming.

creep. (1) In lithography, the movement of the blanket surface or plate packing caused by static conditions or by the squeezing action that occurs during image transfer. (2) The displacement of each page location in the layout of a book signature as a result of folding the press sheet.

crop marks. Small lines placed in the margin or on an overlay, denoting the image areas to be reproduced.

cropping. (1) Indicating what portion of the copy is to be included in the final reproduction. (2) Trimming unwanted areas of a photograph film or print.

cross-direction. The position across the grain, or at a right angle to the machine direction, on a sheet of paper. The stock is not as strong and more susceptible to relative humidity in the cross-direction.

cross-grain. Folding at right angles to the binding edge of a book, or at a right angle to the direction of the grain in the paper stock. Folding the stock against the grain.

cross-web. The position at a right angle to the grain or machine direction of a web of flexible material.

cure. The process of drying ink sufficiently so that it does not adhere to the printer or press. Inks are also cured to prevent blocking and setoff.

curl. Uneven warping of the edges of a sheet aggravated by moisture and affected by the direction of the paper fibers.

cursor. The blinking line approximately the length of one character that, as displayed on a computer screen, marks the current working position in a file and can be moved to any other point in the file by shifting the position of the mouse and clicking on the new position, by clicking on a command in a dialog box, or by executing function key commands.

cyan. A blue-green color, complementary to red. Along with yellow and magenta, one of the three primary subtractive colors, or process colors used in the printing process. Cyan reflects blue and green light, while absorbing red.

cyan printer. (1) The plate used to print the cyan ink in process color reproduction. (2) The negative or positive film or color proof that indicates what image areas will print in cyan.

cylinder. (1) A roller with grippers that hold and press the sheet against the inked form roller on a printing press. (2) Any roller or drum with a continuous or screened circumference used in papermaking. (3) Any of the principal rollers on an offset printing press: plate, blanket, and impression cylinders.

cylinder press. (1) A basic press design in which the form is held on a reciprocating flatbed that moves alternately under the ink rollers and a large rotating cylinder. The cylinder carries the paper, pressing it against the form. (2) A screen printing press in which the substrate, wrapped around a rotating drum, contacts the printing surface of a moving screen and is discharged onto a conveyor after printing. (3) A press used for diecutting.

daguerreotype. A positive image produced on a silver-coated copper plate. The first practical photographic process, it was invented by Louis J. M. Daguerre in 1839. The image is developed by exposing the plate to metallic mercury vapors.

dampeners. Paper, cloth, or rubber-covered rollers that distribute water to the printing plate in the lithographic process.

dampening. Moistening nonimage areas of lithographic plates with water-covered rollers.

dampening fountain. A pan on the press that holds the solution used to wet the plate.

dampening solution. A mixture of water; gum arabic; an acid, neutral, or alkaline etch; and isopropyl alcohol or an alcohol substitute used to wet the lithographic press plate. Alternative term: fountain solution.

dampening system. A series of rollers that moisten the printing plate with a metered flow of a water-based solution containing such additives as acid, gum arabic, and isopropyl alcohol, or other wetting agents.

darkroom. The light-tight chamber in which photographic materials are handled and processed.

darkroom camera. A graphic arts camera constructed so that the rear element, film holder, ground glass, and focusing controls are within the darkroom, permitting the film to be loaded directly without holders.

delivery. (1) The section of a printing press that receives, jogs, and stacks the printed sheet. (2) The output end of bindery equipment.

delivery, dual pocket. A two-tray system on a three-knife trimmer in which a counter activates a switch that directs a specified number of signatures into one tray or the other.

demographic edition. A printed job, usually an advertisement or sections of a magazine, that is targeted toward a specific consumer group within a defined geographic area.

densitometer. An instrument for measuring the optical density of a negative or positive transparency, or of a print. Reflection densitometers measure the amount of light that bounces off a photographic print at a 90° angle. Transmission densitometers measure the fraction of incident light conveyed through a negative or positive transparency without being absorbed or scattered. Combination densitometers measure both reflection and transmission densities.

densitometry. The procedure of measuring optical density and using such measurements to control factors in graphic reproduction.

density. (1) The light-stopping ability of an image or base material, sometimes referred to as optical density. (2) A photographic term used to describe the tonal value of an area. A darker tone has a higher density than a lighter tone. A dry ink film has a higher density than a wet one. (3) The specific gravity or weight per unit volume of paper.

density range. The measured difference between the maximum and minimum densities of a particular film negative or positive.

depth of field. The distance range between the nearest and farthest objects that appear in acceptably sharp focus in a photograph.

descender. The portion of a lowercase type character that extends below the common baseline of a typeface design, such as in "g," "j," "p," "q," and "y."

desensitize. (1) To chemically treat the nonimage areas of a lithographic plate to make them water-receptive and ink-repellent. (2) An agent or dye used to treat exposed photographic plates and films to permit development in brighter light.

desktop publishing. The creation of fully composed pages with all text and graphics in place on a system that includes a personal computer with a color monitor; word processing, page-makeup, illustration, and other off-the-shelf software; digitized type fonts; a laser printer; and other peripherals, such as an optical image scanner. Completely paginated films are output from an imagesetter.

development. (1) The process of converting a latent photographic image on film or paper to a visible image. (2) In lithographic platemaking, removing the unhardened coating from the plate surface.

die. (1) A pattern of sharp knives or metal tools used to stamp, cut, or emboss specific shapes, designs, and letters into a substrate. (2) A plate cut, etched, or embossed in intaglio to provide a raised impression on paper.

die, embossing. A heated or cold brass or steel tool that impresses a design in relief into a paper substrate. Unlike a cutting die, the edge is not sharp.

diecut. A printed subject cut to a specific shape with sharp steel rules on a press.

diecutting. (1) Using sharp steel rules to slice paper or board to a specific shape on a printing press or a specialized stamping press. (2) Engraving dies used in stamping or finishing.

die-stamping. Use of a die of brass or other hard metal to stamp the case of a book. The case may be stamped with ink or metallic foil. If the impression is without color, the case is said to be blind-stamped.

diffraction theory. In halftone photography, dot formations that occur as the result of deflected light.

diffusion transfer. A process used to produce positive screened prints and line prints on paper, film, or lithographic plates by physically transferring the image during processing from an exposed special light-sensitive material (a negative sheet with a silver emulsion) to a sheet of paper, film, or aluminum (the receiver sheet).

digital. Method of representing information in numerical (binary) code. Unlike a continuous analog signal, a digital one is represented by discrete electronic pulses that are either "on" or "off."

digital device. A scanner, computer, or other equipment that uses discrete electronic pulses, signals, or numerical (binary) codes to represent information. The values are stored as a series of ones and zeros.

digital dot. An imaging spot created by a computer and output by a laser printer or imagesetter. Digital dots are uniform in size; halftone dots vary in size.

digitize. To convert an image or signal into binary form.

digitized information. Text, photographs, and illustrations converted into digital signals for input, processing, and output in an electronic publishing system.

direct digital color proof (DDCP). Proof printed directly from computer data to paper or another substrate without creating separation films first. Proof made with a computer output device, such as a laser or ink-jet printer.

direct-to-plate technology. Those imaging systems that receive fully paginated materials electronically from computers and expose this information to plates in platesetters or imagesetters without creating film intermediates.

disk, floppy. A thin, flexible, removable magnetic disk used to store computer data. An example is a high-density 3½-in. computer disk.

disk, hard. A platter-like magnetic storage device often permanently encased in a computer system.

display type. Those type styles and sizes designed mainly for use as headline and advertising matter, instead of as straight text or body composition. Alternative term: display matter.

doctor blade. (1) A steel blade that wipes the excess (surface) ink from a gravure cylinder before printing, or the excess coating from the cylinder during finishing operations. (2) A steel or wooden blade used to keep cylinder surfaces clean and free from paper, pulp, size, or other material during papermaking. (3) A long metal knife blade used to apply or remove ink or coating on a printing press or finishing system. A doctor blade is also used on some flexographic presses to remove ink from the surface of the anilox roll.

dog-ear. A corner or other portion of a page that is misfolded to such a degree that it cannot be corrected by trimming.

dot. The individual element of a halftone. It may be square, elliptical, or a variety of other shapes.

dot area. In photomechanical reproduction, a screen breaks the wide tonal range found in the original into discrete intervals (from 1% to 99%), creating a halftone dot pattern. The value of each increment, or interval, in the halftone is expressed as the percentage of dot area covered.

dot gain. The optical increase in the size of a halftone dot during prepress operations or the mechanical increase in halftone dot size that occurs as the image is transferred from plate to blanket to paper in lithography.

dot pattern. The design formed by the dots in a halftone screen or a screen-printing stencil. The light and dark tones produced by the dots, which vary in size, compose the image.

dot range. The difference between the smallest printable halftone dot and the largest nonsolid-printing dot.

double spread. A printing image that extends across and fills two pages of a brochure, book, or folder. If located in the center of a book or folder, it is called a center spread. Alternative terms: spread, double-page spread, double truck.

doubling. A printing defect in the halftone imaging process that appears as a faint second image slightly out of register with the primary image.

drop initial. Typographic style in which an oversize initial is placed so as to "drop" below the top alignment of the accompanying text setting.

drop shadow. A dark outline in or around portions of typeset letters. The shadow effect is separated from the main body of the letter by space.

drop-on-demand ink jet. A nonimpact printing method in which ink droplets are emitted only when required for imaging. Alternative terms: asynchronous ink jet; intermittent ink jet. See also: bubble jet; valve jet.

drum. (1) An oscillating metal ink distribution roller. (2) A synonym for cylinder in many press applications.

drum scanner. Color separation equipment on which the original transparency is wrapped around a hollow, plastic rotary cylinder.

dry offset. Printing from relief plates by transferring the ink image from the plate to a rubber surface and then from the rubber surface to the paper. Printing with this process on an offset press eliminates the need to use water. Alternative terms: indirect letterpress; letterset; relief offset.

dryer. (1) A unit on a web press that hardens the heatset ink by evaporating the solvent ingredient in it. (2) Any conveyor or static oven used to hasten drying of a wet material by subjecting it to heat generated by gas flame, electricity, or air circulated at an ambient temperature.

drying agent. An ink additive, such as a salt of cobalt or manganese, that acts as a catalyst in converting a wet ink film to a dry ink film.

drying in. Condition that occurs when ink dries prematurely in the meshes of a (screen) printing screen, blocking and clogging the stencil openings. This causes a lack of detail in the printed image.

ductor roller. A cylinder that alternately transfers ink from the ink fountain roller to the ink distribution rollers or dampening solution from the water fountain roller to the dampening rollers on an offset press.

dummy. (1) A preliminary layout showing the position of illustrations, text, folds, and other design elements as they are to appear in the printed piece. (2) A set of blank pages prepared to show the size, shape, style, and general appearance of a book, pamphlet, or other printed piece.

duotone. A special effects technique that consists of making a two-color halftone reproduction from a single-color original. In the most common type of duotone, the two halftones are printed in two different colors—one in a color (a normal halftone negative) and the other in black (to print the lighter-than-normal shadows).

duplex. A press or electronic printer that allows two sides of a sheet to be printed in one pass.

duplicating. (1) A photomechanical process in which an image identical to the original is formed on a photosensitive material. (2) Producing short runs of simple usually single- or two-color printed material on a small press. (3) Preparing identical printing plates to reproduce multiple versions of the same image.

duplicator. Any press that is without bearers and smaller than 11×17 in. (279×432 mm). Duplicators are regularly used to print simple single- or two-color work, but can also be used to print multicolor jobs.

durometer. A measure of a roller or blanket's hardness or softness.

durometer gauge. Instrument used in printing to measure roller hardness.

dusting. The accumulation of visible paper particles on the nonimage areas of the blanket. Alternative term: powdering.

dye. (1) A soluble coloring material, normally used as the colorant in color photographs. (2) Non-pigment coloring agents of mineral or vegetable origin with high penetration characteristics. Often used in decorating textiles.

dye sublimation. A method of proofing in which the images are created by dyes secured to the substrate by heating.

E

electronic color correction. The process of altering, retouching, cloning, combining, silhouetting, smoothing, sharpening, and adjusting tone and color balance or otherwise manipulating color images with an electronic (computer-assisted) imaging system.

electronic color scanner. Equipment that uses beams of light, electronic circuitry, and color filters to examine a color image, point by point, and separate it into films representing each of the three process printing colors (yellow, magenta, and cyan) and black.

electronic composition. Computer-assisted methods of copyfitting and pagination that output text and graphical elements in completed page form as paper galleys or film from an imagesetter.

electronic dot generation. Linking laser with digital technology to produce a halftone dot pattern without a contact screen. A separate digital computer in the laser scanner stores information about the halftone screen, its rulings, and screen angles.

electronic imaging systems. Computer-controlled equipment used to merge, manipulate, retouch, airbrush, and clone images, create tints and shapes, and adjust and correct individual color areas within an image that has been scanned, stored on magnetic disk, retrieved and displayed on the monitor, and positioned according to a predetermined layout.

electronic publishing. Any system using a computer and related word processing and design and page-makeup software to create paginated text and graphics, which are output to a laser printer with a PostScript interpreter and/or imagesetter at varying degrees of resolution from a minimum of 300 dots per inch to maximum quality levels exceeding 1,250 dots per inch.

electrostatic printing. Printing method in which electrically charged, powdered colorant particles are transferred from the image carrier to a substrate moving in their path. The particles are fused to the substrate to form the permanent image.

em. A printer's unit of area measurement equal in width and height to the height of the letter "M" in any selected type body size. Now commonly used as an abbreviation of pica-em, where the em is equivalent to 12 points (approximately one-sixth inch).

em dash. A line one em long that connects interrelated or parenthetical material in typeset text.

em space. A nonprinting fixed space equal in width to the point size of a font. It is used for indenting paragraphs and aligning type columns.

embossing. (1) Using impressed dies to print text or designs in relief on any one of a variety of paper stocks. (2) The swelling of a lithographic offset blanket caused by ink solvent absorption. (3) Undesirable condition resulting from heavy ink coverage in solid image areas on a press sheet. The ink pulls away from the paper as it is peeled from the blanket following impression, causing the solid image areas to appear as high relief images.

emulsion. Photographic term for a gelatin or colloidal solution holding light-sensitive salts of silver in suspension. It is used as the light-sensitive coating on photographic film or plates in photomechanical printing processes.

en. A printer's unit of area measurement equal to the same height but half the width of the em. The en is sometimes used to specify the area of composition as its value closely approximates the number of characters in the text.

en dash. A line one en long that connects interrelated material in typeset text.

en space. A blank space half the value of the em space; usually equal to the width of a numeral in text sizes. It is used for alignment of figure columns and indentions.

enamel. A glossy paper surface coating material.

end leaf. A strong paper manufactured for the specific requirements of combining and securing the body of a book to its case. One leaf is pasted against the book's front cover and one against the back cover. The remaining four, six, or eight pages (flyleaves), which are made of the same heavy stock, separate the case from the text pages. Endpapers are often marbleized or carry other ornamental printed designs.

end matter. The material printed at the end of a book, after the text proper, including appendixes, bibliographies, glossaries, indexes, etc.

end product. The final package or printed piece ready for customer use after all folding, gluing, and other binding, finishing, and/or converting operations are completed.

engraving. (1) In the graphic arts, a metal plate with a relief-printing surface prepared by acid etching or electronic engraving. Line engravings reproduce only solid blacks and whites, while halftone engravings reproduce continuous-tone material as a series of very small dots. (2) An illustration prepared from a metal plate with a relief-printing surface that has been etched with acid or electronically engraved.

enlargement. A reproduction larger than the original itself. The degree of enlargement is specified as a percentage greater than 100%, or a ratio greater than one.

enlarger. A light source, lenses, bellows, and a film holder that are adjusted to project an image larger than the original from a film negative onto a sheet of photographic paper.

etch. (1) To dissolve away with chemicals. (2) The function of increasing or decreasing the density of a continuous-tone image in one or more areas. It can be completed electronically or manually (with chemicals). (3) An acidified gum solution that reacts chemically with nonimage areas not protected by a resist. It is used to produce a relief image on an engraving plate. (4) In lithography, acidic substances, usually in a gum arabic solution, that are used to clean the plate and desensitize nonimage areas to ink, making them receptive to dampening solution (water) instead.

exposure. (1) The period of time during which a light-sensitive surface (photographic film, paper, or printing plate) is subjected to the action of actinic light. (2) The product of the intensity and the duration of the light acting upon a photographic emulsion.

exposure latitude. The range of exposures that will produce acceptable results from a specific film.

exposure meter. An instrument with a light-sensitive cell that measures the light reflected from or falling on a subject. It is used as an aid in selecting the proper exposure setting. Alternative term: light meter.

extension. (1) A three-letter suffix added primarily to DOS and Windows file names to describe the contents of the file. (2) The distance between the lens and the photosensitive material or between the lens and the copyholder in a camera.

fabrics, stencil. Woven webs of materials (natural and synthetic fabrics and fine wire) used as image carriers in screen printing.

feedboard. A platform or ramp on which the sheets to be printed are transported by tapes or vacuum belts to be registered [positioned] by the front stops and side guide, prior to insertion into the impression cylinder grippers by the infeed system.

feeder. (1) A mechanism which separates, lifts, and passes individual press sheets from the top of a pile table onto the feedboard to front stops. The sheets are laterally positioned on the feedboard by a side guide and then fed into the first printing unit. (2) The device that forwards signatures or newspaper inserts, etc., through an in-line finishing system.

felt side. The top side of the paper formed on the paper machine wire. It is the preferred side for printing.

festoon. A method of storing a relatively large amount of paper used for zero-speed splicing on a web press. The festoons also condition the paper, stretching it and removing the curl from the roll.

fiber. Wood particles used in the papermaking process.

file. A collection of digital information stored together as a unit on a computer disk or other storage medium and given a unique name, which permits the user to access the information. A file may contain text, images, video, sound, or an application program.

file server. A workstation primarily responsible for redirecting resources across the network. Dedicated file servers require that the computer running the server software not be used for other tasks. Nondedicated servers permit the administrative tasks and the shared resources to be spread over various network nodes.

filler. Inorganic materials like clay, titanium dioxide, calcium carbonate, and other white pigments added to the papermaking furnish to improve opacity, brightness, and the overall printing surface.

filling up. A condition in which ink plugs up the areas between halftone dots and produces a solid rather than a sharp halftone print. This may also occur in the printing of type matter. Alternative term: plugging.

film. (1) Sheets of flexible translucent or transparent acetate, vinyl, or other plastic base materials that are coated with a photographic emulsion. (2) Any thin, organic, nonfibrous flexible material (usually not more than 0.010 in. thick) that is used as a substrate in flexography. Some examples include cellophane, polyethylene, Saran, acetate, and Mylar.

film image assembly. Positioning, mounting, and securing various individual films to one carrier sheet in preparation for platemaking.

film processors. Machines that treat and develop photographic films and papers with chemicals under controlled conditions to produce permanent visible images.

film speed. Numerical indicator of how sensitive a given film is to light. Films with higher numbers are more sensitive, or respond faster, to exposure.

filter. (1) A colored sheet of transparent material, such as gelatin, acetate, or glass, that is mounted over a camera lens to emphasize, eliminate, or change the color or density of the entire scene or certain elements in the scene. Photographic lenses absorb (filter out) certain wavelengths of light while allowing others to pass through. (2) A transparent material characterized by its selective absorption of certain light wavelengths and used in a variety of applications, for example, to separate the red, green, and blue components of an original when making color separation films.

filter, major. (1) The filter, the color of which is the complement of the subtractive process primary measured. (2) That filter, the color of which is mostly absorbed by any color when compared to the other additive filter primary colors. (3) Of the three primary color filters (red, green, and blue), the filter used to obtain the highest density reading. In most densitometric equations, the major filter reading is denoted by the symbol/letter "H."

filter, major-minor. (1) That additive primary filter (other than the major filter), the color of which is ab-sorbed by any color, causing hue contamination. (2) Of the three primary color filters (red, green, and blue), the filter used to obtain the medium or middle density reading. In most densitometric equations, the major-minor filter reading is denoted by the symbol "M."

filter, minor-minor. (1) That additive primary filter, other than the major filter, the color of which is absorbed by any color, resulting in a gray or achromatic contamination, but not in hue contamination. (2) Of the three primary color filters (red, green, and blue), the filter used to obtain the lowest density reading. In most densitometric equations, the minor-minor filter density reading is denoted by the symbol/letter "L."

finish. The surface characteristics of paper.

finishing. All forms of completing graphics production, including folding, trimming, and assembling sections; binding by sewing, wire stitching, or gluing; and diecutting or gold stamping.

fixer. A solution that makes the developed image on a film permanent. It does so by dissolving or neutralizing the remaining unexposed emulsion.

flagging. (1) Indicating a web splice so that the spliced product can be removed from the press folder and discarded. (2) Marking printed matter to indicate a change or correction. (3) Inserting small strips of paper into a skid of press sheets as needed to indicate segments of defective printed sheets.

flash. A brief, intense burst of light produced by a bulb or an electronic unit, usually used where the scene lighting is inadequate for photography.

flat. (1) A sheet of film or goldenrod paper to which negatives or positives have been attached (stripped) for exposure as a unit onto a printing plate. (2) Description of a print or proof lacking contrast, color, or brilliance.

flatbed. (1) A printing press in which the form is held in a horizontal platen. Flatbed presses are often used as proofing presses. (2) A color scanner on which the original is mounted on a horizontal table instead of a rotary drum.

flat-panel display. A computer monitor illuminated by liquid crystals, gas plasma, or electroluminescence.

flexography. A method of rotary letterpress printing characterized by the use of flexible, rubber or plastic plates with raised image areas and fluid, rapid-drying inks.

flooding. In lithography, excess water on the printing plate or in the ink caused by improper ink/water balance.

flush. (1) Type composition set without paragraph indentions. (2) An ink wetting agent.

flush left. Lines of type composition aligned to the left margin, with a ragged right margin. Alternative terms: quadded left; ragged right; unjustified text.

flush right. Lines of composition aligned to the right margin with a ragged left margin. Alternative terms: quadded right; ragged left.

focal length. The distance between the optical center of a lens and the point at which an object image is in sharp or critical focus.

focal plane. The light-sensitive film or plate on which camera images transmitted by a lens are brought to sharpest focus. The focal plane rests in a fixed position. Alternative term: film plane.

fold. Bending and creasing a sheet of paper as required to form a printed product.

fold marks. Guides on the pasteup that indicate where a printed piece will be creased.

fold plates. Two smooth, flat metal sheets that receive the paper that has come through the buckling mechanism on a folder during binding and finishing.

folder. Machine that creases and scores printed sheets of paper to particular specifications during binding and finishing. The process itself is called folding.

folder, combination. A bindery machine or in-line finishing component of a web press that incorporates the characteristics of knife and buckle folders.

folder, ribbon. A folder on a web press used for publication work. It slits the web into multiple strips of the width required by the desired product size. Each ribbon is turned over an angle bar and guided into position so that all ribbons align with each other ahead of the jaw-folding section. The ribbons of paper are collated and brought down to the cutoff knives and folding jaws in either one or two streams. The press then simultaneously delivers either one or two sets of signatures of the same size. See also: angle bar.

folder dummy. A mockup that shows the placement of page heads, the binding edge, and the gripper and side-guide edges, as well as page sequence and signature arrangement.

foldout. An oversize leaf, often a map, an illustration, or a table, folded to fit within the trim size of a book and tipped (pasted) in.

folio. (1) In printing, a page number, often placed at the outside of the running head, at the top (head) of the page. (2) In descriptive bibliography, a leaf of a manuscript or early printed book, the two sides designated as "r" (recto, or front) and "v" (verso, or back). (3) Formerly, a book made from standard-size sheets folded once, each sheet forming two leaves, or four pages.

folio lap. The additional paper on the side edges of a signature that extend beyond the trim size of the pages. Folio laps are included so that binding equipment can grab and insert the signature into a magazine or book. Alternative terms: high folio; low folio.

font. A complete collection of characters in one typeface and size, including all letters, figures, symbols, and punctuation marks.

footcandle. A unit in which light intensity is measured. It is equal to the intensity of a standard candle at a distance of one foot.

footer. A book's title or a chapter title printed at the bottom of a page. A drop folio (page number) may or may not be included.

form. (1) Either side of a signature. A form usually contains a multiple of eight pages, but may be more or less. (2) Type locked in a chase and ready to be put on a letterpress.(3) In the case of offset, a finished, camera-ready proof may be referred to as a form.

form roller. In lithography, the device that transfers dampening solution or ink from an oscillating roller to the printing plate. Most lithographic presses typically have one or two dampening form rollers and three to five inking form rollers.

formation. The structure and uniformity of a paper's fiber distribution as judged by transmitted light.

former. A smooth, triangular-shaped, metal plate over which a printed web passes prior to entering an in-line folder. The former folds the moving web in half lengthwise.

former fold. First fold given paper coming off a web press, often before the paper is cut into sheets. The former fold is made in the direction of web travel, thus parallel to the grain.

fountain. A reservoir for the dampening solution or ink that is fed to the plate on a lithographic press. Alternative term: water pan.

fountain blade. On an offset press, the strip of flexible steel or plastic angled against the ink fountain roller. The fountain blade acts as a squeegee against the fountain roller allowing only the amount of ink determined by the setting of the ink keys, to remain on the fountain roller to contact the ductor roller.

fountain keys. A series of thumb screws or motor-driven screws or cams behind the fountain blade that provide for variable inking across the ink fountain. The keys control the amount of space between the ink fountain blade and the ink pan roller. The amount of space between the blade and pan roller determines the amount of ink feed from an ink key. Alternative term: ink keys.

fountain leveler. A sensing device, usually mechanical or ultrasonic, that checks the height of the ink moving over the agitator.

fountain roller. A metal roller that rotates intermittently or continuously in the ink or dampening fountain and carries the ink or dampening solution on its metal surface. The variable speed of the fountain roller will increase or decrease the feed overall to the plate. Alternative terms: ink pan roller, water pan roller.

fountain solution. In lithographic printing, a combination of water, gum arabic, and other chemicals used to wet the printing plate and keep the nonimage areas from accepting ink. Some fountain solutions contain alcohol. Alternative term: dampening solution.

four-color process printing. The photomechanical reproduction of multicolor images achieved by overprinting specified amounts and areas of yellow, magenta, cyan, and black inks.

fourdrinier. A paper machine that forms a continuous web of paper on a horizontal, forward-moving, endless wire belt.

frame. (1) The wood or metal construction that supports the screen fabric in screen printing. (2) A block positioned on a page into which the user can place text or graphics.

free sheet. Wood pulp that has been treated with a caustic solution to remove impurities. Paper that is free from groundwood.

French fold. A press sheet in which all of the pages are printed on one side and folded, first vertically and then horizontally, to produce a four-page signature. The blank side is folded inward before the other folds are made.

frontlighting. Light shining on the subject from the direction of the camera.

front matter. The pages preceding the text of a book, including the title and copyright pages, the preface, foreword, table of contents, list of illustrations, and dedication.

f-stops. Fixed sizes at which the aperture of the lens can be set. The values of the f-stops are determined by the ratio of the aperture to the focal length of the lens.

full bleed. An image extending to all four edges of the press sheet leaving no visible margins.

furnish. The mixture of fibrous and nonfibrous materials like fillers, sizing, and colorants in a water suspension from which paper or paperboard is made.

fuser, fuser roll. In electrostatic printing, the component of the toner assembly that is maintained at a high temperature to facilitate toner bonding with the substrate.

gallery. A photography studio.

gallery camera. A process camera extending from the darkroom into the area of the photography studio where "roomlight" operations can be performed.

galley. (1) The raw output of a phototypesetter, usually in the form of single columns of type on long sheets of photographic paper, which serve as preliminary proofs. (2) The final typeset (or imageset) copy output to photographic paper, or directly to film. (3) A long, shallow tray used to store and proof handset type.

gamut. The greatest possible range.

gang. (1) A grouping of different or identical forms arranged to print together in one impression. (2) Multiple photographic images exposed as one unit.

gatefold. A four-page book insert that is larger than some dimension of the page and opens from each side of the center.

gathering. Assembling a set of signatures sequentially. Alternative terms: assembling, collate, insert.

gear marks. Alternating light and dark marks that appear as bands in halftones and solids parallel to the gripper edge of the sheet. The distance between marks is uniform and equal.

gloss. The relative amount of incident light reflected from a surface. Printing papers are often said to have varying degrees of specular gloss.

ghosting, gloss. Condition that occurs during sheetfed printing when the vapors from ink printed on one side of a press sheet chemically interact with the dry ink densities overprinted on the reverse side of the same press sheet or on the next sheet in the pile. The faint, dull images that indicate gloss ghosting usually appear in large shadow or solid areas of the press sheet and develop only when inks containing drying oils are used to print the job. Alternative term: fuming ghosting.

Glossary

ghosting, mechanical. Condition that occurs when the ink film on the press sheet shows abrupt variations in color densities, especially when a narrow solid printed ahead or behind a wider solid consumes much of the ink on the form rollers. Alternative term: ink starvation ghosting.

gloss. The relative amount of incident light reflected from a surface. Printing papers are often said to have varying degrees of specular gloss.

gloss ink. An ink containing varnish or other additives. It dries with a minimum of penetration into the stock and yields a high luster.

glue lap. The area of a printed package or container reserved for the adhesive material used to fasten the folded carton.

gluing-off. Applying glue to the spine of a casebound book after sewing and smashing, but before the book is trimmed.

gradation. The gradual change of tones from one to another in originals, negatives, and reproductions.

grade. A means of ranking paper, film, and other printing supplies.

gradient. A rate of increase or decrease.

grain. (1) The distribution, coarseness, and size of silver particles in photographic emulsions and images. (2) The roughened or irregular surface of a printing plate. (3) In papermaking, the machine direction, or the direction in which the fibers lie.

grain, with the. Binding term in which paper is folded parallel to the direction of the paper grain.

grain direction. (1) In papermaking, the alignment of fibers in the direction of web travel. (2) In printing, paper is said to be "grain-long" if the grain direction parallels the long dimension of the sheet. The paper is referred to as "grain-short" if it parallels the short dimension of the sheet. (3) In book binding, the grain direction of all papers used must run parallel to the book backbone.

grain direction, across. Method of printing at right angles to or opposite the paper grain direction.

grain direction, against. Folding or cutting paper at right angles to the paper grain in the direction of the sheet's fibers.

graininess. The sand-like or granular appearance of a negative, print, or slide resulting from irregularly distributed silver grains that clump together during film development. Graininess becomes more pronounced with faster films, increased density in the negative, and degrees of enlargement.

graphic communications. Allied industries, including printing, publishing, advertising, and design, that participate in the production and dissemination of text and images by printed or electronic means.

graphical user interface (GUI). A visual way to represent computer commands and objects on screen. The user interacts with the computer by selecting icons and menu items from the screen, usually by moving and clicking with a mouse.

graphics. Artwork, photographs, and charts that are reproduced or presented in visual form.

gravure. An intaglio printing process in which minute depressions, sometimes called cells, that form the image area are engraved or etched below the nonimage area in the surface of the printing cylinder. The cylinder is immersed in ink, and the excess ink is scraped off by a blade. When paper or another substrate come in contact with the printing cylinder, ink is transferred.

gray. (1) Any of a series of neutral colors ranging between black and white. The tint or color formed by blending black and white in varying proportions. (2) When a surface reflects a comparative ratio of each light wavelength in the visible spectrum at a relatively low combined intensity the human eye perceives gray.

gray balance. The values for yellow, magenta, and cyan that produce a neutral gray with no dominant hue when printed at a normal density.

gray balance chart. Near-neutral yellow, magenta, and cyan dot values printed in a grid pattern. A halftone black gray scale is used as a reference to find the three-color neutral areas. The dot values that compose these areas represent the gray (color) balance requirements for a set of color separations. The gray balance chart should be produced in-house under normal production conditions using the process inks, paper, plates, and press that will be used for the job.

grayness. An attribute calculated from density readings that relates to the degree of three-color contamination in a cyan, magenta, or yellow process color ink. As grayness values increase, an ink exhibits lower saturation or purity.

gray scale. A reflection or transmission film strip showing neutral tones in a range of graduated steps. It is exposed alongside originals during photography and used to time development, determine color balance, or to measure density range, tone reproduction, and print contrast. Gray scales can also be used to check focus and resolution. Alternative terms: gray wedge; neutral gray wedge; step tablet; step wedge.

gripper. (1) The metal clamps or fingers located on impression cylinders and transfer cylinders, that grasp and hold a sheet while being transported through a printing press. (2) The reference edge of a layout, film flat, or print plate that corresponds to the sheet edge held by the grippers on the press.

groundwood. Pulp produced during papermaking by grinding bark-free logs against a revolving stone in the presence of water. It is used principally in newsprint and lower grades of book paper.

guide edge. The side of a sheet at right angles to the gripper edge that is used to control the lateral (side-to-side) position of the sheet as it travels through the press or folder.

guide side. The area on the press that controls the position of the sheet during printing. It is usually the side closest to the press operator.

guillotine cutter. A manual or electronic device with a long, heavy, sloping blade that descends to a table or bed and slices through a stack of paper.

gum. (1) In lithography, a water-soluble colloid, such as gum arabic or cellulose gum, that desensitizes the nonimage areas on a printing plate, making them ink repellent. It is also used to preserve the plate for future use. (2) A general term referring to natural, resinous binders that are used in the formulation of inks and varnishes.

gutter. In typography, the inside margin (white space) between facing pages or columns of type. In bookbinding, the margin at the binding edge. Alternative terms: gutter margin; back margin.

H

halation. (1) A photographic term used in platemaking to describe light that spreads beyond the sharp definition of an image. Poor contact between the negative flat and the negative-working plate during platemaking distorts the image by allowing light to expose nonimages areas, causing a blurred effect. Dirt, masking materials, or tape prevents proper contact between the film negative and the plate. (2) Poor contact between the negative flat and the negative-working plate during platemaking that distorts the image by allowing light to expose nonimage areas, causing a blurred effect. Dirt, masking materials, or tape prevents proper contact between the film negative and the plate. In positive platemaking, dot loss occurs.

halftone. A printed reproduction of a continuous-tone image composed of dots that vary in frequency (number per square inch), size, or density, thereby producing tonal gradations. The term is also applied to the process and plates used to produce this image.

halftone screen. A sheet of glass or film that is used as an intermediate between continuous-tone copy and photosensitive material. Continuous-tone images are exposed to the photosensitive material through the screen's regular arrangement of transparent and opaque areas. This produces an image pattern of small, solid dots (or narrow lines) that vary in size (or width) and represent tonal gradations. Halftone screens with higher screen rulings (e.g., 133 lines/in. as opposed to 65 lines/in.) produce higher resolution images.

head. (1) A line of display type signifying the title of a work or conveying crucial information. A headline. (2) The top of a page, book, or printing form. (3) A compact device that reads, scans, writes, or records data on a surface medium, particularly the fixed or moving electromagnetic elements used for reading and writing data on magnetic tapes, disks, and drums.

header. A book's title or a chapter title printed at the top of a page and often with a folio (page number). Alternative term: running head.

hickey. An imperfection on a printed sheet caused by dirt, hardened ink, or other unwanted particles that cling to the press, blanket, or plate during lithographic printing. Hickeys appear as either a small, solid printed area surrounded by a white halo, or an unprinted spot surrounded by printed ink.

high key. A photographic or printed image in which the predominant detail lies in the highlights.

high-contrast image. The relationship of highlights to shadows in continuous-tone or halftone photography, i.e., the darker portions of the image are uniformly very dark; the lighter portions are uniformly very light; and the midtone range is nonexistent or very small.

highlight. The lightest or whitest area of an original or reproduction, represented by the densest portion of a continuous-tone negative and by the smallest dot formation on a halftone and printing plate.

hot melt. (1) A molten wax or plastic adhesive material that is applied with a roller or knife or through the casting or extrusion method at elevated temperatures in liquid form. It solidifies upon cooling and imparts high gloss and good barrier properties to paper and board. (2) A bookmaking glue that is solid at room temperature and must be heated to achieve liquidity.

hot-metal. Type produced by casting molten metal to form individual characters or slugs.

hue. A visual property determined by the dominant light wavelengths reflected or transmitted.

hue, primary. (1) Any three hues, normally a red, a green, and a blue, so selected from the spectral scale as to enable a person with normal color vision to match any other hue by the additive mixture in varying proportions. Alternative terms: physical primary hues/colors; physical color primaries. (2) In the subtractive color process, the primary hues are yellow, magenta, and cyan; those transparent inks/colors that absorb only (or mostly) the additive primaries of blue, green, and red, respectively.

hydrophilic. Water-receptive.

hydrophobic. Water-repellent.

I

illustrations. Drawings, sketches, graphics, photographs, etc., used in conjunction with printed matter.

image. (1) Any picture, drawing, subject, or reproduction visible to the human eye that portrays the original in the proper form, color, and perspective. (2) A picture formed by light. The optical counterpart of an original focused or projected in a photographic camera.

image analysis. Use of a television camera connected by a digitizing board to a computer for the study of patterns and other geometric measurements on a sample image. Ragged edges may also be judged with an image analyzer.

image area. On a lithographic printing plate, the area that has been specially treated to receive ink and repel water.

image carrier. The device on a printing press that carries an inked image either to an intermediate rubber blanket or directly to the paper or other printing substrate. A direct-printing letterpress form, a lithographic plate, a gravure cylinder, and a screen used in screen printing are examples of image carriers.

image fit. The agreement in distance between the register marks on each color from the gripper to the tail edge of the press sheet.

imagesetter. A device used to output fully paginated text and graphic images at a high resolution onto photographic film, paper, or plates.

imposetter. A device used to output fully imposed signatures at a high resolution onto photographic film, paper, or plates.

imposition. Assembling the various units of a page before printing and placing them on a form so that they will fold correctly. Alternative term: image assembly.

imposition layout. A guide that indicates how images should be assembled on the sheet to meet press, folding, and bindery requirements.

imposition systems. Step-and-repeat imaging cameras or computerized methods of assembling the units of pages into signatures for printing. The latter method is sometimes referred to as electronic imposition.

impression. (1) The printing pressure necessary for ink transfer. (2) A single print.

impression cylinder. In lithography, the hard metal cylinder that presses the paper against the inked blanket cylinder, transferring the inked image to the substrate. The impression cylinder on most sheet-fed presses uses paper grippers to hold the sheet through its rotation.

inch. To move the printing press slowly; small degrees of movement.

indicia. Permit information for the post office as printed on a "self-mailer" brochure, magazine, or label.

infeed. (1) The section of a sheetfed press where the sheet is transferred from the registering devices of the feedboard to the first impression cylinder. (2) The set of rollers controlling web tension ahead of the first unit on a web press.

initial letter. A large capital or otherwise decorated character that begins a chapter or paragraph.

ink. A printing ink is a dispersion of a colored solid (pigment) in a liquid, specially formulated to reproduce an image on a substrate.

ink drum. A metal roller in the ink distribution system of a press that moves back and forth sideways to help mix the ink and reduce ghosting. Alternative terms: oscillator; vibrator.

ink fountain. The trough on a printing press that holds the ink supply to be transferred to the inking system. The operator controls ink volume from adjustment screws or keys on the fountain or from a remote console. The ink fountain consists of an ink reservoir, ink keys, an ink pan or fountain roller.

ink tack. The sticky or adhesive quality of an ink which is measured by determining the force required to split an ink film between to surfaces.

ink-dot scum. On aluminum plates, oxidation characterized by scattered pits that print sharp, dense dots, or ink material trapped in the grain.

ink-jet printing. A nonimpact printing process in which a stream of electrostatically charged microscopic ink droplets are projected onto a substrate at a high velocity from a pressurized system. The electrically controlled flow of droplets is either intermittent or continuous.

ink/water balance. In lithography, the appropriate amounts of ink and water required to ink the image areas of the plate and keep the non-image areas clean.

in-line finishing. Manufacturing operations such as numbering, addressing, sorting, folding, diecutting, and converting that are performed as part of a continuous operation right after the printing section on a press or on a single piece of equipment as part of the binding process. In-line finishing is common in web printing operations.

insert. (1) In stripping, a section of film carrying printing detail that is spliced into a larger film. (2) In printing, a page that is printed separately and then bound into the main publication. (3) Assembling signatures one inside of another in sequence.

intaglio. Any form of printing in which the image areas are engraved or etched below the nonimage areas on the printing plate or cylinder to provide ink-retaining reservoirs or wells. Gravure is considered an intaglio printing process.

intermediate. (1) A contact print from an original negative or positive. (2) A print made from the key layout to produce a set of blueline flats for stripping.

internegative. Negative made from a transparency (positive) to generate photographic prints. Prints made from internegatives are of higher quality than prints made directly from transparencies, but lower in quality than those made directly from a first-generation negative.

isopropyl alcohol. A component of lithographic dampening solution that makes it easier to obtain ink/water balance and reduces the water surface tension so that it covers the nonimage areas of the plate more evenly. Less dampening solution is carried to the blanket because isopropyl alcohol evaporates so rapidly.

italic. A slanted version of a typeface with vertical lines that are between 8° and 20° from the perpendicular to the character baseline. In typeset copy, italic type is used to signify periodical titles and other special information.

jaw folder. Three cylinders in the in-line finishing area of a web press that make one or two parallel folds at right angles to the direction of web travel. Alternative terms: parallel folder; tucker folder.

jog. To align flat, stacked sheets or signatures to a common edge, either manually or with a vibrating table or hopper. Some in-line finishing systems are equipped with a jogger-stacker that piles and aligns folded signatures as they are delivered.

joggers. Two movable devices in the delivery of a sheetfed press that work along with the rear sheet guide and a front gate to align and stack printed press sheets.

justification. The process of composing a line of type by spacing between the words and characters to fill an exact measure, thus aligning the type at both margins. Hyphenation is sometimes employed to achieve justification. In other cases, only the spacing between words is adjusted.

K

Kelvin. A unit of temperature equal to 1/273.16 of the Kelvin scale temperature of the triple point of water.

Kelvin temperature scale. A thermometric scale on which the unit of measurement equals the Celsius degree and according to which absolute zero is 0 K, the equivalent of −273.15°C. Acceptable viewing conditions in the graphic arts are measured in Kelvin.

kerning. Manipulating type character widths and white space to achieve aesthetically pleasing results.

key. (1) The master layout or flat that is used as a positioning guide for preparing color artwork and/or stripping other film flats. The key is usually prepared from the black printer but may include detail from other colors where registration marks do not appear in the black. Alternative term: key flat. (2) In photography, the emphasis on lighter or darker tones in a negative or print. High key indicates the prevalence of light tones; low key the prevalence of darker tones.

kiss impression. The minimum pressure at which proper ink transfer is possible.

knife. (1) In folding machines, the three or four blades at different levels and at right angles to each other that force the paper between the folding rollers. The sheet of paper is pushed from one knife folding mechanism to the other until the desired number of folds have been made. (2) A sharp steel blade that trims excess from sheets and/or cuts them to a specific size. Automatic trimmers and cutters have knifes that can be programmed to make precise cuts.

knockout. Type that appears as white on a black or dark colored background. Alternative terms: reverse; dropout.

kraft. A thick, usually brown paper or cardboard made from unbleached sulfate wood pulp. It is often used as bag and wrapping paper.

L

laminate. A product made by bonding together two or more layers of material, usually with an adhesive.

lap. (1) The edge where one color overprints another. Alternative term: bleed. (2) The extra edge on one side of a signature gripped by binding equipment during the inserting process.

laser. A high-energy, coherent (single-wavelength) light source. The small spot of light produced by the laser makes it possible to expose light-sensitive and photoconductive materials at high speed and high resolution.

laser printer. A nonimpact output device that fuses toner to paper to create near-typeset quality text and graphics. The basic technology is similar to that of a photocopier.

laser scanner. A device that uses color filters, electronic circuitry, and beams of light to produce tone- and color-corrected separations from color originals mounted on rotating drums.

latent image. The invisible reproduction retained in an exposed photographic emulsion. Development converts the latent image to a visible image.

layout. A guide prepared to show the arrangement and location of all the type, illustrations, and line art that are combined together to compose the film flat.

layout, rough. A drawing developed from a thumbnail sketch, but more detailed and larger.

leader. A character consisting of two or more dots set in a row. Leaders are inserted between text on the left- and right-hand sides of a line. In lists, directories, tables of contents, etc., the leader guides the eye from the left-hand text to the right-hand text in the line.

leading. The amount of space between the baseline of one line of type and the baseline of the adjacent line. The space is inserted to separate the type characters on the two lines.

leaf. (1) A separate, usually blank, sheet of paper in a book. (2) A pigmented stamping material used to decorate book edges.

lens. An optical device consisting of glass elements mounted in a barrel that collect and distribute light rays to form an image.

letter fold. Creasing a sheet several times in the same direction with two or more creases wrapping around the inner leaf.

letterpress. The method of printing in which the image, or ink-bearing areas, of the printing plate are in relief, i.e., raised above the nonimage areas.

letterset. An offset letterpress printing process. The relief image on the letterpress plate is first transferred to a rubber blanket and then to paper. Unlike offset lithography, this process does not require a dampening system. Alternative term: dry offset.

library binding. A book bound in conformance with the specifications of the American Library Association. The requirements include stitched signatures, sewn-on four-cord thread, strong endpapers, muslin-reinforced endpapers, and flannel backlining extended into the boards.

light. Electromagnetic energy with wavelengths (about 380 to 750 nm) that affect vision.

light integrator. A device that measures the intensity and duration of an illumination source. A combination of a timer and a light meter, it is used to determine and control uniform film or plate exposures.

light meter. A device used to determine the correct exposure for negatives, positives, and color transparencies. It has three scales; one set for the speed of the emulsion used and one set to the meter reading of the illumination source. The correct exposure (in seconds or fractions of a second) is read from the third scale opposite the various apertures (lens openings) that can be used.

light sensitive. A material that is chemically altered after it is exposed to light.

light spectrum. The electromagnetic wavelengths, typically measured in nanometers, that are visible to the human eye. Each color in the light spectrum has a different wavelength.

light table. A glass-topped work area illuminated from underneath and used for pasting up layouts, stripping, opaquing, and otherwise viewing images with transmitted light.

lightfastness. The ability of a printed substrate to resist deterioration (fading and yellowing, etc.) caused by sunlight or artificial light.

lighting. The illumination falling on a subject, particularly the direction or arrangement of the illumination.

line art. A drawing with no grays or middletones. Traditionally, black lines on white paper. In computer publishing, an object-oriented graphic. While scanned-in line art is bitmapped, line art created (mathematically) in the computer is a vector, or object-oriented, graphic.

lines per inch. Designates the resolution of a halftone screen. Screens with a higher number, such as 120 or 133, have a higher resolution than screens with lower numbers, such as 65 lines per inch. Alternative term: screen ruling.

lip. In saddle-stitched binding, the extended edge of one side of a signature that is gripped to open the signature to the center spread to facilitate inserting.

liquid-crystal display. A monitor in which images are formed by a liquid crystal material.

lithography. A printing process in which the image carrier is chemically treated so that the nonimage areas are receptive to water (i.e., dampening or fountain solution) and repel ink while the image areas are receptive to ink and repel water. The image carrier is said to be planographic, or flat and smooth.

lithography, waterless. A planographic printing process that relies on special surface properties of the printing plate, instead of a water-based dampening solution, to prevent ink from adhering to nonimage areas of the plate. The nonimage areas of this "waterless" plate consist of an ink-repellent silicone rubber layer. The process also requires special inks and temperature-controlled inking systems.

logotype. A ligature, special symbol, trademark, trade name, or any other combination of characters, words, or phrases produced as a single graphic and allocated a given width in a typesetting system.

loose register. Term used when each color image on a press sheet is relatively independent of all others and slight variations in press register are inconsequential.

loose-leaf binding. A process in which individual sheets can be inserted and removed at will from a section of a larger document often held in a three-ring binder.

loupe. An adjustable-focus magnifier incorporating a precise measuring scale, with or without a self-contained light source. It is used to inspect fine detail.

lowercase. The uncapitalized letters of the alphabet. Originally called lowercase because the lead type version was located in the lower portion of the California Job Case. Alternative term: minuscules.

M

machine direction. The grain position, or the direction that the sheet moved as it was formed in the papermaking machine.

magenta. The subtractive transparent primary color that should reflect blue and red and absorb green light. It is one of the four process-color inks used in the printing process.

magenta printer. (1) The plate that prints magenta ink. (2) The color separation film that will be used to produce the magenta printing plate.

makeready. All of the operations necessary to get the press ready to print a job.

makeup. Assembling text, illustrations, graphs, charts, rules, tabular material, and running heads or feet into a completed page. Stripping, pasteup, and electronic pagination are all forms of makeup. Alternative term: page layout.

marks. The lines on films, flats, printing plates, and press sheets that serve as guides for positioning, registering, printing, and binding a job.

markup. Indicating the typographic specifications for a job, including type style and size, format and spacing directly on the manuscript.

master. (1) The original from which subsequent copies are made. (2) The final copy (paginated film or paper) upon which all changes have been made and approved before printing.

master page. The page in a computer pagination program on which all headers, rules, and other elements that will repeat on all of the pages of a document are set.

masthead. Information identifying the title, ownership, management, subscription rates, and other pertinent information concerning a newspaper or periodical. Alternative term: flag.

matte. A flat, dull, slightly roughened surface that scatters the specular component of light and causes any underlying tones to appear lighter. A matte surface lacks gloss or luster.

mechanical. The assembly of all page elements, including text and line art, properly proportioned and positioned, in camera-ready form. Alternative term: pasteup.

metameric. A color that changes hue under different illumination sources.

metamerism. The process in which a change in an illumination source will cause visual shift in the hue of a color.

micrometer, dead-weight. A device that uses the unrelieved weight of an anvil to obtain repeatable measurements from plates, blankets, and packing.

midtone dot. A point in a middle-gray area of a halftone. Its area equals or approaches the average of the nearby background areas. Together all midtone dots have a checkerboard-like appearance.

midtones. The range of tonal values between halftone highlight and shadow areas. Alternative term: middletones.

misregister. Printed images that are incorrectly positioned, either in reference to each other or to the sheet's edges.

moiré. An undesirable, unintended interference pattern caused by the out-of-register overlap of two or more regular patterns such as dots or lines. In process-color printing, screen angles are selected to minimize this pattern. If the angles are not correct, an objectionable effect may be produced.

monochromatic. A single color or shades of a single color.

movable type. The individual metal or wooden type characters that are taken from the typecase, arranged to form words and sentences, and then returned to the case for reuse later.

multicolor press. Two or more connected printing units (each with its own inking and dampening system), a feeder, a sheet transfer system, and a delivery. Two or more colors can be printed on one side of a sheet during a single pass through the press.

multimedia. Combining more than one means of providing information—text, audio, animation, and full-motion video—for use as a teaching tool, in a presentation, or for entertainment purposes. CD-ROMs are often used to store the enormous amount of data necessary to create and run a multimedia product.

Munsell color system. A method of classifying surface color in a solid. The vertical dimension is called value, the circumferential dimension is called hue, and the radial dimension is called chroma. The colors in the collection are spaced at subjectively equal visual distances.

N

negative. A photographic film or plate that is exposed and processed to provide a reversed image of the tones found on the original—highlights and shadows or color values (i.e., white as black).

nip. (1) The line of contact between two press cylinders. (2) A crease line at the joint of a case-bound book. It gives books uniform bulk and reduces the swelling caused by the sewing thread. See also: smash.

nippers. In bookbinding, the flat irons on a "building-in" machine or casing-in line. When heated, the nippers clamp the book joint, joining the case and the book at the base.

nipping. In binding, squeezing and clamping books or signatures after sewing or stitching to remove excess air and reduce the swell caused by stitching. Hard papers are nipped and soft papers are smashed.

nonimage area. The portion of a lithographic printing plate that is treated to accept water and repel ink when the plate is on press. Only the ink-receptive areas will print an image.

nonimpact printer. A printing device that creates letters or images on a substrate without striking it. Large, high-speed and ordinary office photocopiers, as well as laser and ink-jet printers are just some examples.

nonprocess printing. Color printing in which the desired color is achieved by using an ink of that color (such as a PMS color) instead of yellow, magenta, and cyan (the process colors).

notch binding. Small serrations cut in the spine of a perfect-bound book and filled with glue. This method eliminates the need to mill material off the spine of the book.

octavo. A sheet folded to form 8 leaves or 16 pages, or a book prepared from sheets so folded. The page size varies with the sheet dimensions, but this binding term is sometimes used to designate a page that is approximately 8X5 in.

offline converting. Coating, cutting, folding, embossing, stamping, or otherwise altering newly printed sheets or rolls of material to form the final printed piece or product on a machine separate from the printing press. Printing plants may have dedicated converting equipment or they may send the work to companies that specialize in converting.

offset gravure. A printing process in which the gravure image carrier (usually a cylinder) transfers ink to a rubber blanket that deposits the ink on the surface to be printed. Offset gravure is used to achieve special printed effects on metal surfaces and, in combination with flexography, to print on flexible packages.

offset printing. An indirect printing method in which the inked image on a press plate is first transferred to a rubber blanket, that in turn "offsets" the inked impression to a press sheet. In offset lithography, the printing plate has been photochemically treated to produce image areas and nonimage areas receptive to ink and water respectively.

OK sheet. A press sheet that closely matches the prepress proof and has been approved by the customer and/or production personnel. It is used as a guide to judge the quality of the rest of the production run.

oleophilic. Oil-receptive, as in the image areas of a lithographic printing plate.

oleophobic. Oil-repellent, as in the dampened nonimage areas of a lithographic printing plate.

on-demand printing. A method of producing a select number of documents at a given time by storing a publication electronically. It is easier to update and modify documents more frequently and print additional copies at a later date without incurring new start-up costs. Excessive inventories are also eliminated.

opacity. The degree to which light will not pass through a substrate or ink.

opaque. Any material that will not permit the passage of light.

open. (1) Slightly underexposing and developing a halftone negative so that the printed illustration will be fuller and darker than the original because the halftone dots formed are somewhat larger than would normally be obtained. (2) A word used to characterize the visual appearance of typographic matter that is widely spaced or surrounded by large amounts of white space. This effect is used to avoid the dense, block-like appearance of solid masses of type.

optical character recognition (OCR). A technique in which any printed, typed, or handwritten copy or graphic images are scanned by an electronic reader that converts the information into a form that can be read, interpreted, and displayed by computers.

original. Any artwork, mechanical, photograph, object, or drawing that is submitted to be reproduced in the photomechanical process.

orphan. The first line of a paragraph that is also the last line on a page or column, generally considered poor typography. Sometimes, the last line of a paragraph which is also the first line on a page is referred to as an orphan.

oscillator. A gear-driven roller that not only rotates, but moves from side to side, distributing and smoothing out the ink film and eliminating image patterns from the form roller. This side-to-side movement reduces mechanical ghosting.

overcorrection. Removing too much of a contaminating color when correcting color separations for the hue error present in the printing inks. The result is a loss of important detail in the final reproduction.

overdevelop. To subject exposed photographic material to a developing solution for excessive time or at excessive temperature, agitation, or concentration.

overprint. A color made by printing any two of the process inks (yellow, magenta, and cyan) on top of one another to form red, green, and blue secondary colors.

overrun. The quantity of printed copies exceeding the number ordered to be printed. Trade custom allows a certain tolerance for overruns and underruns.

overtrapping. In process color printing, the transfer of an excessive amount of one color over another.

packing. (1) The procedure for producing the pressure between the plate and blanket cylinders in offset lithography. (2) The paper or other material that is placed between the plate or blanket and its cylinder to raise the surface to printing height or to adjust cylinder diameter to obtain color register in multicolor printing.

page description language (PDL). In an electronic publishing system, the format by which all of the elements to be placed on the page, their x-y coordinates (respective position on the page), and the page's position within the larger document are identified in a manner that the output device can understand.

page layout. A dummy indicating page size; trimmed job size; top, outside, and foot trims; untrimmed page size; and head, foot, outside, and bind margins.

page makeup. (1) A computer program that allows the user to position type and other elements automatically so that fully paginated electronic output can be generated. (2) Manual placement of art, type, photos, etc. into page positions by adhering each element to a "board" ready for camera work.

pagination. (1) The process of page makeup. (2) Numbering pages with associated running heads and feet, sometimes including trim marks. (3) Breaking down an electronic file or printed galley into individual pages.

Pantone Matching System (PMS). The most commonly used ink-mixing and color-reference formula, a trademark of Pantone, Inc.

paper. Matted fibers, usually made from wood, applied to a fine screen from a water suspension to form thin sheets.

paper, uncoated. Paper that has not been treated or processed with a surface coating during manufacture. The rougher surface absorbs inks more readily.

paper basis weight. In the United States, the weight in pounds per ream of paper cut to its basic size. The size varies with different grades and varieties of paper. It also varies from country to country.

paper sizes, international. The common paper sizes used in Europe and Japan. They are: A3 (11.7×16.5 in.); A4 (8.3×11.7 in.); A5 (5.8×8.3 in.); B4 (10.1×14.3 in.); B5 (7.2×10.1 in.); and B6 (5.1×7.2 in.).

paperboard. A paper product with a greater basis weight, thickness, and rigidity than paper. With a few exceptions, paperboard has a thickness of 12 points (0.3 mm) or more.

paperbound. An adhesive-bound book with a paper cover.

passive-matrix display. A monitor that uses a single transistor to control an entire column or row of electrodes. These displays are cheaper than active-matrix displays, but provide lower contrast and resolution.

paster. (1) A device used to apply a fine line of paste on either or both sides of the web to produce finished booklets directly from the folder without saddle stitching. The paste is applied from a stationary nozzle as the web passes underneath it. (2) An eight-, twelve-, or sixteen-page booklet that is pasted instead of saddle-stitched together. (3) An automatic web splicer on a press. (4) The rejected web with a splice in it.

perf strip. A band that is bound into saddle-stitched publications so that single-leaf inserts can be tipped in. If perf strips were not used, publications could only accept four-page inserts. Alternative term: hangers.

perfect binding. The use of glue to hold the pages of a book or magazine together. Alternative term: adhesive binding.

perfecting. Printing both sides of a sheet in the same pass through the press. In xerography, perfecting is called duplexing.

perfecting press. A printing press that prints both sides of a sheet in a single pass through the press.

perforating. Punching a row of small holes or incisions into or through a sheet of paper to permit part of it to be detached; to guide in folding; to allow air to escape from signatures; or to prevent wrinkling when folding heavy papers. A perforation may be indicated by a series of printed lines, or it may be blind; in other words, without a printed indication on the cutline.

Photo CD™. A format developed by Kodak for storing compressed still photographic images on CD-ROM disks. The digital photographs can be viewed on home players or can be retrieved with computer-based systems. See also: CD-ROM.

photocopy. A reproduction of an original formed by fused toner particles in a nonimpact process such as xerography.

phototypesetting. The act of composing type and reproducing it on photographic film or paper.

pica. A printer's unit of linear measure, equal to approximately one-sixth of an inch. There are twelve points in a pica and approximately six picas in an inch.

pick-up. Film, photos, or type from a previously printed job that is earmarked for reuse in an upcoming job.

pigment. Fine, solid particles derived from natural or synthetic sources and used to impart colors to inks. They have varying degrees of resistance to water, alcohol, and other chemicals and are generally insoluble in the ink vehicle.

piling. A buildup of paper, ink, or coating on the offset blanket, plate, or rollers in such a quantity that it interferes with print quality. Alternative term: caking.

pin register. The use of standardized register pins and holes to ensure accurate register of copy, film, and plates during prepress; especially for process-color printing.

pixel. Picture element. The smallest tonal element in a digital imaging or display system.

planographic. A term used to describe a flat image carrier, such as a lithographic printing plate, which has no relief images and has image and nonimage areas on the same level (or plane).

plate. A thin metal, plastic, or paper sheet that serves as the image carrier in many printing processes.

plate clamp. A device that grips the lead and tail edges of a printing plate and pulls it tight against the cylinder body. The position of the clamps is relevant to the image position or register of the image in relation to the other printing plates and the images squareness on the sheet.

plate cylinder. In lithography, the cylinder that holds the printing plate tightly and in register on press. It places the plate in contact with the dampening rollers that wet the nonimage area and the inking rollers that ink the image area, then transfers the inked image to the blanket, which is held on its own cylinder.

plate scanner. A device that measures all of the various densities in a plate's image area at selected increments across the plate before it is mounted on the press. The press operators then set the ink fountain keys to match the ink densities indicated by the plate scanner's measurements before they begin printing the job.

platemaking. Preparing a printing plate or other image carrier from a film or flat, including sensitizing the surface if the plate was not pre-sensitized by the manufacturer, exposing it through the flat, and developing or processing and finishing it so that it is ready for the press.

platen. In letterpress, a movable flat surface that is pressed firmly against paper and inked type to produce a printed image.

platen press. A printing press with a flat printing surface and a flat impression surface.

"pleasing" color. Printed color subjective in nature (e.g., flesh tones, sky, etc.). Alternative terms: reference color; memory color.

pockets. The hoppers on a binder that are loaded with the signatures to be bound into a book.

point. (1) The smallest American unit of typographic linear measurement, equal to 0.0138 in. Type height is measured in points. (2) Units of measure that indicate the caliper of paper in thousandths of an inch.

point size. Specifying the height of the body of a typeface in units of linear measure equal to 0.0138 in.

point system. The system of measuring by points and picas in typographic composition. It has been in use in the United States since 1878.

pop-ups. A sheet that is diecut, creased, and folded in two directions. It is flattened for delivery and, when opened, expands to form a three-dimensional image.

position proof. A color proof in which text, graphics, and pictures are combined and checked for location and registration before printing.

positive. A photographic reproduction with the same tonal values as those in the original scene. The image areas on the film or plates are represented by opaque dot values.

portable document format (PDF). A computer file format that preserves a printed or electronic document's original layout, type fonts, and graphics as one unit for electronic transfer and viewing. The recipient uses compatible "reader" software to access and even print the PDF file.

positive. A photographic reproduction with the same tonal values as those in the original scene. The image areas on the film or plates are represented by opaque dot values.

posterization. A special effects photographic technique that renders continuous-tone copy into an image represented by a few broad, flat, dark middletones and shadow areas. All highlight and light middletone areas are eliminated.

PostScript™. Adobe Systems, Inc. tradename for a page description language that enables imagesetters developed by different companies to interpret electronic files from any number of personal computers ("front ends") and off-the-shelf software programs.

PostScript™, encapsulated. A file format used to transfer PostScript™ image information from one program to another.

preflighting. An orderly procedure using a checklist to verify that all components of an electronic file are present and correct prior to submitting the document for high-resolution output.

prepress. All printing operations prior to presswork, including design and layout, typesetting, graphic arts photography, image assembly, and platemaking.

prepress proofing. Producing a simulation of the final printed piece by photochemical methods (such as an overlay of dye or pigment images on transparent film base) instead of photomechanical methods (ink on paper).

press. The machine that creates the final printed image.

press gain. Mechanical dot gain.

pressrun. (1) The total of acceptable copies from a single printing. (2) Operating the press during an actual job.

presswork. All operations performed on or by a printing press that lead to the transfer of inked images from the image carrier to the paper or other substrate. Presswork includes makeready and any in-line finishing operations specific to the press (folding, perforating, embossing, etc.).

primaries. Colors that can be used to generate secondary colors. In the additive system, these colors are red, green, and blue. In the subtractive system these colors are yellow, magenta, and cyan. The printing process employs the subtractive color system.

print. (1) In photography, an image made by reproducing a negative (or positive) on a sensitized opaque support of paper, metal, or other materials. (2) The line or halftone image on metal plates used in photomechanical printing processes. (3) An impression from a plate, engraving, etc.

printability. The combination of print quality characteristics that enhance the reproduction of an original in any printing process.

printer. (1) Any computer device that produces results in readable form on paper. (2) Color-separated halftone films that will transfer the characteristics of each specific process color in a given job to the corresponding printing plate prior to presswork. (3) The person or company that operates printing presses.

printer, impact. Any device that uses pressure from a typebar, type head, or matrix pin and inked ribbon to strike a direct impression on a substrate.

printer, nonimpact. Any device that reproduces an image without striking the substrate. Some examples include xerography or laser printing in which the image is created by fused toner particles, or ink jet printing in which a stream of ink propelled from the printer forms the image.

printing. The art and methods by which an original is reproduced in quantity. In the photomechanical process, this is generally accomplished by applying an inked image carrier to the substrate as it travels through a high-speed press.

printing process. The method used to reproduce written and pictorial matter in quantity. The major conventional printing processes are lithography, letterpress, gravure, flexography, and screen printing. The major nonimpact printing processes are ink jet, electrophotography, ionography, magnetography, and thermal transfer printing.

printing screen. The frame, fabric, and stencil assembly used in screen printing.

printing unit. The sections on printing presses that house the components for reproducing an image on the substrate. In lithography, a printing unit includes the inking and dampening systems and the plate, blanket, and impression cylinders.

process colors. The three subtractive primary colors used in photomechanical printing (cyan, magenta, and yellow, plus black).

process inks. The yellow, cyan, magenta, and black colorants that, when combined in a photomechanical printing process, reproduce four-color images.

proof. A prototype of the printed job made photomechanically from plates (a press proof), photochemically from film and dyes, or digitally from electronic data (prepress proofs). Prepress proofs serve as samples for the customer and guides for the press operators. Press proofs are approved by the customer and/or plant supervisor before the actual pressrun.

proof, progressive. A set of press proofs from the separate plates used in process color work, showing the printing sequence and the result after each additional color has been applied. (Press proofs of each individual process color and black; each combination of two process colors; each combination of three process colors; and all four process inks combined.) Alternative term: progs.

proof, soft. An intangible image, such as that on a computer screen, not as reliable as a traditional proof.

proof press. A printing machine used to produce photomechanical proofs. It has most of the elements of a true production machine but is not meant for long pressruns.

proofing. Producing simulated versions of the final reproduction from films and dyes or digitized data (prepress proofing) or producing trial images directly from the plate (press proofing).

proofreader. A person who checks copy for errors and marks them for correction prior to printing.

proofreaders' marks. A series of symbols and abbreviations used by a proofreader to mark errors on copy and the corrections to be made.

quality system. The organizational structure, responsibilities, procedures, processes, and resources that printers use to control the many printing variables in order to generate products of consistent quality that meet defined specifications.

quartertone. Picture tonal values in range of a 25% dot.

quarto. (1) A sheet folded into four leaves or eight pages. (2) A booklet, or the pages of a book, formed by folding the sheets into four leaves, with a final size usually measuring about 12×9½ in.

quick printing. Category of printers that provide a fast turnaround of short-run jobs.

rag content. The percentage of cotton fiber in paper.

ragged. Type composition set with lines centered in the column, instead of justified, producing raggedness at both sides.

raster. An image composed of a set of horizontal scan lines that are formed sequentially by writing each line following the previous line, particularly on a computer monitor or television screen.

raster image processor (RIP). The device that interprets all of the page layout information for the marking engine of the imagesetter. PostScript™, or another page description language, serves as an interface between the page layout workstation and the RIP.

rasterization. The process of converting mathematical and digital information into a series of dots by an imagesetter for the production of negative or positive film.

ream. Five hundred sheets of paper.

recto. The right-hand page of an open book, usually an odd-numbered page; sometimes the first or cover page.

recyclable paper. Wastepaper or stock separated from other solid waste and designated for reuse as a raw material. Papers that are heavily contaminated (with color or coating) may not be recyclable.

recycled paper. Paper manufactured from deinked used paper and bleached pulp or from printing and converting waste.

reducer. (1) An additive that softens printing ink and reduces its tack. (2) A chemical that reduces the density of a photographic image by removing silver.

reference colors. Those colors to which the eye most readily responds including flesh tones, green grass, and blue sky. Alternative term: memory colors.

reflectance. The ratio between the amount of light reflected from a given tone area and the amount of light reflected from a white area.

reflection. An optical term for the direction change of a ray of light when it falls on a surface and is thrown back into the medium from which it approached.

reflection copy. A photographic print, painting, or other opaque copy used as original art for reproduction. Such copy is viewed by the light reflected from its surface and can only be photoreproduced with front illumination (as from a graphic arts camera) as opposed to the backlighting used to view and reproduce transmission copy (i.e., slides and transparencies).

register. The overall agreement in the position of printing detail on a press sheet, especially the alignment of two or more overprinted colors in multicolor presswork. Register may be observed by agreement of overprinted register marks on a press sheet. In stripping, film flats are usually punched and held together with pins to ensure register. The punched holes on the film flat match those on the plate and press specified for the job.

register, commercial. In process-color reproduction, the degree of acceptable misregister, usually no more than one-half of a row of dots. Ultimately, the customer determines what constitutes acceptable misregister.

register marks. Small reference patterns, guides, or crosses placed on originals before reproduction to aid in color separation and positioning negatives for stripping. Register marks are also placed along the margins of negative film flats to aid in color registration and correct alignment of overprinted colors on press sheets.

register plate. A device that stops the lateral (sideways) movement of the sheet on the feedboard of a lithographic press. Alternative term: register block.

register punch. The device used to cut holes and insert register pins into film flats and plates during prepress so that they remain in position. The holes and register pins used in prepress must be standardized to suit the particular press on which the job will be printed to ensure accurate alignment throughout the run.

relief plate. A metal, rubber, or photopolymer printing plate on which the image areas are raised above the nonimage areas.

relief printing. A printing process using an image carrier on which the image areas are raised above the nonimage areas.

reprography. Copying and photoduplicating type and images by any one of several processes, including xerography, in quantities below the commercial printing level.

resist. A plate coating that hardens over the nonimage areas after exposure to light. Mixed with bichromated gum or other coating solutions, the resist keeps the plate developer from contacting the nonimage areas of the metal plate, while etching it slightly.

resolution. The precision with which an optical, photographic, or photomechanical system can render visual image detail. Resolution is a measure of image sharpness or the performance of an optical system. It is expressed in lines per inch or millimeter.

retouching. Altering continuous-tone prints and halftone negatives or positives to eliminate defects, emphasize detail, and perform minor color corrections. Pencils or dyes were originally used to retouch actual prints, negatives, and positives manually. Today, images are scanned into computerized prepress systems and retouched electronically.

roll. Paper or cardboard produced in a continuous strip and wound uniformly around a central shaft or hollow core.

roller. (1) On printing presses, a cylindrical drum on an axle. Composed of metal or rubber, it distributes and applies ink to the printed form. (2) The cylinders used to convey the paper web through the press or papermaking machine.

roll-to-roll printing. Printing webs of substrates and then rewinding them directly onto another roll core after printing.

rotary drum. An infeed system on a sheetfed press in which the front guides stop the sheet and move out of the way at the proper time. Grippers on a rotating drum clasp each sheet and transfer it to the impression-cylinder grippers.

rotary press. A printing press in which the printing plate or surface is cylindrical and rotates and prints continuously, usually at high speed, on both web and sheetfed stocks.

rotary screen press. A screen printing press with a fine-wire cylindrical screen that contains a squeegee-like blade which rotates over a continuous roll of paper.

rotogravure. A printing process that uses a cylinder as an image carrier. Image areas are etched below nonimage areas in the form of tiny sunken cells. The cylinder is immersed in ink, and the excess ink is scraped off by a blade. When the substrate contacts the printing cylinder, ink transfers, forming the image.

rule. (1) A printed line, usually specified by its arrangement and thickness or "weight," such as hairline, 2-point, 6-point, or parallel. (2) A stamping die used in bookbinding to form borders, panels, etc.

ruling pen. A mechanical pen used for inking lines.

runnability. The mechanical strength of paper. How well it resists tearing during the pressrun.

S

saddle stitch. Binding multiple sheets by opening the signatures in the center and gathering and stitching them with a wire through the fold line. The folded sheets rest on supports called saddles as they are transported through the stitcher. Booklets, brochures, and pamphlets are most often bound this way.

saddle-sewn. Binding multiple sheets on a saddle stitcher with a thread instead of a wire.

safelight. A darkroom light with a limited spectral composition that inhibits it from exposing or fogging specific light-sensitive materials.

sans serif. Typeface designs, such as Helvetica, that lack the small extensions on the ascenders and descenders referred to as serifs.

saturation. (1) The degree to which a chromatic color differs from a gray of the same brightness. In other words, how a color varies from pastel (low saturation) to pure (high saturation). In the Munsell system, this is called chroma. (2) The quality of visual perception that permits a judgment of different purities of any one dominant wavelength.

scan. The sequential examination or exposure of a character or pictorial image with a moving light beam.

scanner. (1) An electronic device that uses a light beam to examine color transparencies and isolate each process color on an individual piece of film, or photographic separation, to be used in the reproduction process. (2) Flatbed electronic devices are used in conjunction with desktop publishing systems to scan line art, logos, photographs, and, with optical character recognition (OCR) capabilities, typewritten or printed text supplied by the client. After the artwork, photographs, and text have been scanned into the system and stored on disk, they are called up on the computer screen and manipulated and assembled in page form using software and then output as a single unit (on paper or film) from the imagesetter.

score. To compress or crease cardboard, pasteboard, or heavy paper along the fiber line to facilitate folding or tearing.

screen. (1) Those areas of a plate or press sheet in which tonal gradations are reproduced. (2) The porous mesh, synthetic, or silk material used as an image carrier in the screen printing process.

screen frequency. The number of lines or dots per inch on a halftone screen.

screen printing. A printing process in which a squeegee forces ink through a porous mesh, synthetic, or silk image carrier, or screen, covered by a stencil that blocks the nonimage areas. The ink pressed through the open image areas of the screen forms the image on the substrate.

screen tint. A halftone film with a uniform dot size throughout. It is rated by its approximate printing dot size value, such as 20%, 50%, etc.

screen value. The number of lines per square inch on any halftone, tint, or four-color separation.

screening. (1) The process of converting a continuous-tone photograph to a matrix of dots in sizes proportional to the highlights and shadows of the continuous-tone image. Screening is usually accomplished photographically by imposing a halftone screen directly in front of the photographic emulsion that will receive the screened image. (2) In gravure printing, the objectionable screen pattern that appears in the solids if cylinder or plate cell walls are excessively shallow or wide.screening in continuous tones. Screen printing with several colors of ink, or inks of several hues, which have been mechanically combined on the printing screen so that each blends smoothly without creating a demarcation line.

scum. Condition that occurs in lithography when the plate has become sensitized in the nonimage areas and these areas begin to take ink.

secondary colors. Colors that are produced by overprinting pairs of the primary subtractive colors. The subtractive secondary colors are red, green, and blue. Alternative term: overprint colors.

sensitize. (1) To make the image areas of a printing plate more ink receptive. (2) To apply a diazo coating, to an aluminum (wipe-on) plate.

separation filters. The red, green, and blue filters used during color separation. Each filter transmits about one-third of the spectrum.

sepia. A photographic print with a brownish tint.

serif. The short, usually perpendicular line found at the end of the unconnected or finishing stroke of a character. Serifs may vary in weight, length, and shape, and contribute greatly to the style of the typeface.

setoff. Condition that results when wet ink on the surface of the press sheets transfers or sticks to the backs of other sheets in the delivery pile. Sometimes inaccurately referred to as "offset."

sewing. In bookbinding, fastening printed signatures together with needle and thread or cord.

shade. (1) In ink manufacture, a common synonym for hue. (2) In some color reproduction systems, the gradations of color resulting from the addition of a small amount of black or a complementary color.

shadow. The darker or denser areas of an original, film positive, or halftone reproduction.

sheet. A piece of paper of a certain size usually used in presswork.

sheetfed press. A printing press that feeds and prints on individual sheets of paper (or another substrate). Some sheetfed presses employ a rollfed system in which rolls of paper are cut into sheets before they enter the feeder; however most sheetfed presses forward individual sheets directly to the feeder.

sheetwise imposition. A printing layout in which separate plates (and film flats) are used to print the front and the back of a single press sheet. Completely different pages appear on each side of the sheet.

shrink wrap. Using heat to affix a thin plastic material around printed and bound products to prepare them for shipment.

side guide. A device that serves as the third point of a three-point register system (including the front guides) on the feedboard. Side guides move the sheet sideways to facilitate register.

side-sewing. A book binding method in which the entire book is sewn as a single unit, instead of as individual sections. Side-sewn books will not lie flat when open.

side-stitch. A method of binding in which the folded signature or cut sheets are stitched along and through the side close to the gutter margin. The pages cannot be fully opened to lie flat.

signature. One or more printed sheets folded to form a multiple page section of a book or pamphlet. Signatures are most commonly grouped as four, eight, sixteen, or thirty-two pages. Various combinations of multiple page signatures create the full complement of pages needed in the printed piece.

silver halide. A silver salt such as silver chloride, silver bromide, and silver iodide suspended in gelatin to prepare the emulsion of photographic film.

skid. (1) A platform on which paper is packed for delivery to or from the pressroom. (2) Any quantity of paper packed on a skid. Standard skids usually contain in excess of 3,000 pounds of paper.

slitter. A sharp rotary blade used to separate a single moving sheet or web into narrow strips, frequently during folding.

slug. (1) A complete line of type cast in a single piece of metal. (2) The single tag line that refers a newspaper reader to a story that is continued on another page. (3) In gravure, the term used to describe cylinder cells that are printing blurred or unclear.

Smyth sewing. Bookbinding by sewing thread through the backfold of a signature and from signature to signature. This links the signatures together, while permitting the opened book to lay flat.

solvent. (1) A material, usually a liquid, capable of dissolving another substance, usually a solid, to form a solution. (2) A component of the vehicle in printing inks that disperses the pigment and keeps the solid binder liquid enough for use in the printing process.

Specifications for Nonheatset Advertising Printing (SNAP). A set of standards for color separations and proofing developed for those printing with uncoated paper and newsprint stock in the United States.

Specifications for Web Offset Publications (SWOP). A set of standards for color separation films and color proofing developed for those involved in publications printing. The SWOP standards help magazine printers achieve accuracy when color separations from many different sources are printed on one sheet.

spectrum. The series of color bands formed when a ray of light is dispersed by refraction; the rainbow-like band of colors resulting when a ray of white light is passed through a prism.

spectrum, electromagnetic. The entire range of wavelengths or frequencies of electromagnetic radiation extending from gamma rays to the longest radio waves, including visible light.

spectrum, visible. The range of wavelengths of the electromagnetic spectrum—from about 400–700 nanometers—that cause the sensation of vision. See also: prism; white light.

spine. The back, or bound, edge of a book.

spiral binding. A mechanical binding method in which a continuous wire coil is run through a series of closely spaced holes near the gutter margin of loose sheets.

splice. The area where two paper rolls are joined to form a continuous roll.

spline. In an image file, the digital representation of a line or curve in terms of coordinates or other symbols, instead of a raster representation. The spline designation is equivalent to vector.

spot color printing. The selective addition of a nonprocess color ink to a printing job.

spread. (1) A line image with edges that have been moved slightly outward to allow a color or tint to intentionally overlap. (2) An image that extends across two facing pages in a book or magazine, crossing over the binding.

squeegee. (1) A rubber or plastic blade used to force ink through the open areas of a screen-printing stencil and mesh to form an image on the substrate. (2) A blade used to sweep solution from printing plates during manual processing.

stacker. A device attached to the delivery conveyor of a web press that collects, compresses, and bundles printed signatures.

stamping. Using a die and often colored foil or gold leaf to press a design into a book cover, a sheet of paper, or another substrate. The die may be used alone (in blank stamping) if no color or other ornamentation is necessary. Special presses fitted with heating devices can stamp designs into book covers.

stamping die. Deeply etched or engraved brass or zinc relief plates used to impress designs on book covers. Brass plates are used when the stamping process requires heat.

stencil. In screen printing a material that, when adhered to the screen, blocks the mesh to keep ink from reaching the nonimage areas of the substrate.

step-and-repeat. Exposing multiple images onto a single film or a single printing plate from a single negative or positive flat. Special step-and-repeat contact frames, projection platemaker, and multi-imaging cameras are used to automate this process.

stitch. Binding printed matter by piercing the pages and securing them together with wire or thread.

stochastic screening. A halftoning method that creates the illusion of tones by varying the number (frequency) of micro-sized dots (spots) in a small area. Unlike conventional halftoning, the spots are not positioned in a grid-like pattern. Instead, the placement of each spot is determined as a result of a complex algorithm that statistically evaluates and distributes spots under a fixed set of parameters. With first-order stochastic screening, only the number of dots in an area varies, but with second-order stochastic screening, both the number and size vary. Alternative terms: FM dots; FM screening.

stock. The paper or other substrate to be printed.

stone lithography. The original form of lithography in which an image is drawn on limestone with wax or grease. The surface of the limestone has been treated so that the nonimage areas accept water and repel the wax or grease.

stripping. The act of combining and positioning all of the copy elements from all of the film negatives or positives together as a negative for platemaking. Alternative term: image assembly.

subhead. A secondary title or heading that is usually set in smaller type, making it less prominent than a main heading.

substrate. Any base material with a surface that can be printed or coated.

subtractive color process. A means of producing a color reproduction or image with combinations of yellow, magenta, and cyan colorants on a white substrate.

subtractive primaries. The colors cyan, yellow, and magenta. Each is formed when one third of the spectrum is subtracted from white light. See also: additive primaries.

T

tabloid. The newspaper page size, approximately 11¾ in. wide and from 15 to 17 in. long, or about half of the standard newspaper page size.

tagged image file format (TIFF). A file format for exchanging bitmapped images (usually scans) between applications.

tear sheet. A job sample torn from a book or newspaper, sometimes with corrections or changes marked on it.

tertiary. Those colors obtained by mixing two secondary colors.

text. The body matter of a page composed in column or paragraph form. Display matter, headings, and illustrations do not fall into this category.

thermal printer. A nonimpact printer that uses heat-sensitive paper to form the image. The paper passes over a matrix of heating elements that act to change its color.

thermography. Raised printing created by heating freshly printed ink that has been coated with a special powder.

thixotropy. The property that causes lithographic inks to become fluid when worked and to return to a semi-solid state later.

three-color process printing. A method of printing in which it is theoretically possible to reproduce all of the hues found in an original by using three separate printing plates, each recording one of the primary colors found in the original. These plates usually are made from three halftone color separation negatives or positives.

throughput. The capacity of a printing system to deliver printed products, usually expressed in sheets per hour, impressions per hour, feet per minute, pages per minute, or square feet per hour.

tint. An image element with an even shading produced by either a halftone dot screen of various shapes and sizes or fine parallel lines. Tints produced with halftone dot screens are often used to measure dot area, dot gain, and print contrast while tints produced with parallel lines are used to measure slur.

tinting. Ink pigment particles that bleed into the dampening solution causing an overall tint to quickly appear on the unprinted areas of the sheet. This tint may appear on the nonimage areas of the plates but can be washed off with water and a sponge; however, it reoccurs when printing is resumed.

tip-in. Using an adhesive to attach a leaf, illustration, or foldout to a book.

tone. The degree of lightness or darkness in any given area of a print.

tone compression. The reduction in density (or tonal range) that occurs naturally in the printed reproduction of an original. It is possible to compensate for it, to improve the quality of the reproduction.

tone reproduction. A comparison of the density of every tone in a reproduction to the corresponding densities on the original.

toner. (1) The electrostatically charged carbon particles suspended in a liquid solvent that fuse to the substrate with heat during photocopying and laser printing, forming the printed image. (2) The powder or liquid used to form images in some color proofing systems. (3) The pigment or dye used to darken the value of an ink color.

trade customs. The business terms, policies, and industry guidelines codified by trade associations for printers and service bureaus. This information provides the starting point for developing contracts and estimates.

transmission copy. A slide or transparency used as original art for reproduction. Such copy is viewed by the light transmitted through its surface and can only be photoreproduced with back illumination.

transparency. A positive photographic record of an image, frequently a color slide, on film.

trapping. (1) Printing a wet ink over a previously printed dry or wet ink film. (2) How well one color overlaps another without leaving a white space between the two or generating a third color.

trim. The excess area of a printed form or page in which instructions, register marks, and quality control devices are printed. The trim is cut off before binding.

trim margin. The white space on the open side of a signature.

trim marks. Guide marks on the original copy and the printed sheet to indicate where the sheet will be cut.

trim size. The final dimensions of a page.

trimmer, three-knife. A cutting machine with three knives, two parallel and one at a right angle, used to trim books or booklets. It operates automatically, usually at the end of a saddle stitcher, perfect binder, or casebound book binding system.

two-on binding. Term used to describe two books trimmed one on top of the other.

two-up. Printing two identical pages on the same press sheet, usually by exposing the plate twice to the same negative.

two-up binding. Binding two units at a time, then cutting them apart and trimming them.

type. The letters, numerals, and special figures produced in different faces and sizes by various composition methods.

type family. A set of typefaces derived from one basic design, e.g., the bold, italic, and condensed variations of the original face.

type styles. A system of general classifications for type, as distinguished by four divisions: Roman, Italic, Script, and Gothic.

typeface. A distinctive type design, usually produced in a range of sizes (fonts) and variations, including bold and italic.

typesetter. (1) A machine that composes type according to certain standardized specifications. (2) The person who sets type.

typesetting. Composing type into words and lines in accordance with the manuscript and typographic specifications.

typesetting, digital. Imagesetters and third-generation phototypesetting machines that eliminate the need for film fonts by storing digital codes in the computer unit and producing type characters as microscopic dots.

typo. An unintentional error made during the keyboarding of a job.

typography. The art and craft of creating and/or setting type professionally.

ultraviolet (UV) curing. Using ultraviolet radiation to convert a wet coating or printing ink film to a solid film.

ultraviolet radiation. The range of electromagnetic radiation (light wavelengths of 200 to 400 nanometers) that lies outside the visible spectrum. In printing, UV rays are used to induce photochemical reactions.

uncoated. A paper stock that has received no mineral applications.

undercolor. In process printing, the yellow, magenta, and cyan present in dark, neutral tones.

uniformity. The consistency of color reproduction and printing quality from unit to unit as one sheet passes through a press.

vacuum frame.
A device that holds film or plates in place by withdrawing air through small holes in a rubber supporting surface. Alternative terms: contact printing frame; vacuum back.

variable printing.
A function of ink jet printers and some typewriters and computer software programs in which specific, changeable information such as names, addresses, and other personalized messages can be inserted or merged into a standardized printed document, such as an advertisement or sweepstakes entry form.

varnish.
(1) A thin protective coating applied to a printed sheet to protect the image and improve appearance. (2) The major component of an ink vehicle, consisting of solvent plus a resin or drying oil.

vector file.
An electronic file that describes geometric shapes and dimensions in terms of coordinates or other symbols.

vectors.
Mathematical descriptions of images and their placement. In electronic publishing, vector graphics information is transferred from a design workstation to a raster image processor (RIP) that interprets all of the page layout information for the marking engine of the imagesetter. PostScript, or another page description language, serves as an interface between the page layout workstation and the RIP.

vehicle.
The liquid component of a printing ink.

Velox.
A photographic print prepared from a halftone negative. It is placed on pasteups and photographed with line copy, eliminating the need for further screening or stripping operations. Velox is a trade name for an Eastman Kodak photographic contact printing paper.

verso.
The reverse, back, or left-hand side of a page, folded sheet, book, or cover.

view file.
A low-resolution electronic file containing the actual data used to form the final output page. Its primary use is to drive (display an image) on the workstation's color monitor. The view file can be output to continuous-tone material to provide a low-resolution proof of a quality slightly better than that displayed on the workstation monitor.

viewing conditions.
A set of American National Standards Institute (ANSI) specifications that dictate the conditions under which originals (transparencies and reflection prints), proofs, and reproductions are viewed. For the graphic arts, the standard specifies a color temperature of 5000 K (a light level of approximately 200 footcandles), a color-rendering index of ninety, and, for viewing transparencies, a neutral gray surround. Large-format transparencies must be viewed with 2–4 in. of white surround and should never be viewed with a dark surround. It is also necessary to view the original or reproduction at an angle to reduce glare.

vignette.
(1) A halftone, drawing, or engraved illustration in which the background gradually fades away from the principal subject until it finally blends into the nonimage areas of the print. (2) An image segment with densities varying from highlight to white. (3) Any small decorative illustration or design used to ornament a book, periodical, or other printed matter, especially before the title page and at the ends of sections or chapters.

viscosity.
A measure of how well a printing ink, glue, or other fluid resists flowing. Viscosity is the opposite of fluidity.

volatile organic compound (VOC).
Any organic compound that significantly participates in photochemical reactions. Presence in emissions (pounds/day) by which clean air standards are measured (e.g., 15 pounds VOC emissions per day). The cleaning solvents used in the printing industry are among those chemical substances that are subject to governmental regulations regarding safety hazards because of VOC emissions.

warm color.
A color that is reddish or yellowish. Red, yellow, and orange are regarded as warm colors.

warp.
The direction of maximum strength on an offset blanket. The warp is indicated by lines across the back of the blanket. To minimize stretching, the blanket is mounted on the press with the warp running around the cylinder.

water stop.
One of a series of devices that are set against the surface of a dampening roller on an offset press. Water stops are commonly used in conventional dampening systems to reduce or meter the amount of dampening solution reaching lightly inked areas of a printing plate.

water-based ink. An ink containing a water-soluble or water-dispersible resin instead of petroleum derivatives.

web. A roll of any substrate that passes continuously through a printing press or converting or finishing equipment.

web offset. A lithographic printing process in which a press prints on a continuous roll of paper instead of individual sheets.

web press. A rotary press that prints on a continuous web, or ribbon, of paper fed from a roll and threaded through the press.

webfed. A printing press that prints on a continuous roll of paper instead of individual sheets.

weft. The direction of minimum strength on a web offset blanket.

white. (1) The presence of all colors. (2) The visual perception produced by light in which each wavelength has the same relative intensity in the visible range as sunlight.

white component. The portion of wavelengths of other colors that dilutes, or desaturates, a saturated color.

white light. The visual sensation that results when the wavelengths between 400 and 700 nm are combined in nearly equal proportions.

white space. The area in printed matter that is not covered by type and illustrations.

widow. (1) Any objectionably short line at the end of a paragraph or headline. It may be expressed as anything less than four characters, less than a full word, less than a certain percentage of the line measure, or any other subjective definition. (2) Any single line on the top of a page.

wire side. The side of a sheet of paper that was formed in contact with the wire of the paper machine during manufacturing.

work-and-tumble. An imposition (layout) in which the front and back of a form is printed from a single plate. After the first run through the press, the stock pile is inverted so that the back edge becomes the gripper edge for the second printing. Work-and-tumble differs from work-and-turn in that the gripper edge changes, often leading to misregister unless the stock has been accurately squared. Alternative terms: work-and-flop; work-and-roll.

work-and-turn. A common printing imposition or layout in which all the images on both sides of a press sheet are placed in such a way that when the sheet is turned over and the same gripper edge is used, one half of the sheet automatically backs up the previously printed half. When the sheet is cut in half parallel to the guide edge, two identical sheets are produced. Work-and-turn impositions are preferred over work-and-tumble impositions for accuracy because the same gripper edge and the same side of the press sheet are used to guide the sheet twice through the press.

work-and-twist. A method of imposition in which a film flat produces two different images on a plate. After the first exposure, the flat is rotated 180° to produce the second exposure.

wraparound. (1) A folio or insert placed around a signature prior to stitching and binding. (2) An increased gutter allowance for the outside pages of larger (32-, 48-, and 64- page) signatures to compensate for creep. See also: creep; shingling. (3) Method of printing from thin copper plates fastened around a plate cylinder in sheetfed gravure.

wrong-reading image. In Western countries, printed type that reads from right to left, or an image printed backwards from its normal orientation. Wrong-reading film images are read from right to left when the film is viewed from the base side.

WYSIWYG (what-you-see-is-what-you-get). Computer screen displays that approximate the true size and true shape of typographic characters, rules, tints, and graphics.

Glossary

X-Y-Z

X-Acto knife. Trademark for a sharp-edged tool used to cut galleys, film, etc.

x-coordinate. (1) The horizontal location of data on a graph, computer monitor, or page layout. (2) The horizontal distance from a selected reference point. Alternative term: x-axis.

xerography. An electrostatic, nonimpact printing process in which heat fuses dry ink toner particles to electrically charged areas of the substrate, forming a permanent image. The charged areas of the substrate appear dark on the reproduction, while the uncharged areas remain white.

x-height. A term used to describe the body height of a type character. It is expressed as the total character height without ascenders or descenders. The letters "x" and "z" from each typeface are selected to serve as examples of the face body height because they rest on the baseline and vary less in height than curved letters.

y-coordinate. (1) The vertical location of data on a graph, display monitor, or page layout. (2) The vertical distance from a selected reference point. Alternative term: y-axis.

yellow. The subtractive transparent primary color that should reflect red and green, and absorb blue light. One of the process-color inks.

yellow printer. In process color printing, the plate used to print the yellow ink image, or the film used to produce the plate that prints the yellow image.

zero-speed splicer. An automatic device that attaches a new roll of paper to an expiring roll without a press stop. The device is used in conjunction with a festoon to permit the expiring roll to come to a complete stop just before the splice is made and then to accelerate the new roll up to press speed.

About the Authors

Sally Ann Flecker

is a writer living in Pittsburgh, Pennsylvania. She is the editor of the award-winning *Pitt Magazine* at the University of Pittsburgh. She has received awards for writing and editing from the Council for the Advance and Support of Education, Women in Communications, the International Competition for Print Advertising and Design, the Public Relations Society of America, the International Association of Business Communicators, the Educational Press Awards, and the International Mercury Awards.

Pamela Groff

is a senior technical writer for the GATF*Press*. In addition to editing *Glossary of Graphic Communications*, she is coauthor of *Understanding Electronic Communications: Printing in the Information Age* and the author of the GATF*World* magazine series "The Internet for Printers." Since receiving her bachelor's degree in English and business administration from La Roche College, she has studied digital media at the University of Pittsburgh's Graduate School of Library and Information Science. She has represented GATF on the Executive Committee of the Student Publications Board of Directors at the University of Pittsburgh for the past six years.

About GATF

The Graphic Arts Technical Foundation is a nonprofit, scientific, technical, and educational organization dedicated to the advancement of the graphic communications industries worldwide. Its mission is to serve the field as the leading resource for technical information and services through research and education.

For 74 years the Foundation has developed leading edge technologies and practices for printing. GATF's staff of researchers, educators, and technical specialists partner with nearly 2,000 corporate members in over 65 countries to help them maintain their competitive edge by increasing productivity, print quality, process control, and environmental compliance, and by implementing new techniques and technologies. Through conferences, satellite symposia, workshops, consulting, technical support, laboratory services, and publications, GATF strives to advance a global graphic communications community.

The GATF*Press* publishes books on nearly every aspect of the field; learning modules (step-by-step instruction booklets); audiovisuals (CD-ROMs, videocassettes, slides, and audiocassettes); and research and technology reports. It also publishes *GATFWorld*, a bimonthly magazine of technical articles, industry news, and reviews of specific products.

For more detailed information on GATF products and services, please visit our website http://www.gatf.org or write to us at 200 Deer Run Road, Sewickley, PA 15143-2600 (phone: 412/741-6860).

GATF Membership Application

GATF members enjoy benefits such as:

- GATF*World* subscription (bimonthly)
- *Technology Forecast* (annual)
- Discounts on books (20%)
- Free technical inquiry hotline
- Discounts on GATF workshops

Name _____

Address _____

City_____ State_____ Zip _____

Country _____

Phone (_____) _____ Fax (_____) _____ Email_____

Membership Classification:

☐ Professional—$75   ☐ Teacher—$40   ☐ Student—$30

Method of Payment:

☐ Check ☐ Visa ☐ Mastercard ☐ American Express ☐ Discover

Signature _____

Print name as it appears on card _____

Card No. | | | | | | | | | | | | | | | | | | | Expiration Date | | | | | | |

Which best describes your primary job interest?
- ☐ Graphic art/design
- ☐ Communications/publishing
- ☐ Marketing/Sales
- ☐ Production ☐ Prepress
- ☐ Press
- ☐ Finishing
- ☐ Production Management
- ☐ Professional/Staff
- ☐ Consultant

Please mail or fax payments to:
Graphic Arts Technical Foundation
Attn: Marketing Group
200 Deer Run Road
Pittsburgh, PA 15143-2600

info@gatf.org   **1-800/910-GATF or 412/741-6860**   **412-741-2311**

GATFPress: Selected Titles